How Do I Get Unstuck

Overcome Internal Resistance, Get Out of Your Own Way, Go After the Life You Want

By Vishnu of Vishnu's Virtues

Copyright © 2019 Vishnu of Vishnu's Virtues
All rights reserved

"Growth is painful. Change is painful. But nothing is as painful as staying stuck somewhere you don't belong." Mandy Hale

For weekly posts on overcoming inner resistance and living the life that is possible for you, check out my articles on Medium at
https://medium.com/@VishnusVirtues

Contents

Introduction 1

1. The Inner Resistance 5
2. Where Does Resistance Come From? 9
3. How Being Stuck Affects Your Life 15

Part 1. Overcoming Internal Resistance 19

4. A Radical Shift to Less 21
5. Small Steps to Overwhelm 27
6. Break the Rhythm 31
7. Inquire Within 35
8. Know How You Work 39
9. Stop Resisting Resistance 43

Part 2. Get Out of Your Own Way 49

10. Thought Clarity 51
11. Intentional Feelings 59
12. Your Beliefs or Your Barriers 65

13. Face Your Fears 71

14. Feeling Worth and Healing Wounds 77

15. Notice the Excuses..83

16. Bounce Back From Your Failures 87

17. Find Your Inner Motivation 93

Part 3. Go After the Life You Want 99

18. Connect With Your Life's Purpose 101

19. What Is Your Life's Message?.....................................105

20. Become Your Own Coach 111

21. Craft Your Ideal Day Today 115

22. Live in Alignment With Your Principles..................119

23. Allow for Being 123

24. Use "No" as Your Superpower...................................127

Get Off the Floor and Get Going...................................131

About the Author 134

Introduction

This is not one of those books that tell you to jump up and down on stage, get motivated, go achieve your dreams and make millions of dollars.

There are plenty of books like that.

There are Instagrammers, YouTubers and motivational speakers who will make you jump out of bed and run towards destiny like your hair is on fire.

If you need to blast off and make a major life overhaul, try another book.

What is this book about?

This is a book about me lying on the floor on my sleeping bag with my laptop a few feet away from me.

Why the sleeping bag? Ha – I gave up the bed!

Why the laptop? It's the place where I write.

Why on the floor? 'Cause I'm down, stuck and can't move!

I'm paralyzed and the thing is, I don't know by what.

This is a book for people who want to go after their dreams but who feel stuck, paralyzed and disempowered. They can't move.

You know that you have the ability but you just can't get it done.

The internal resistance is so strong that it prevents you from achieving the very thing that you want in life.

The only thing between you and the life you want for yourself ... is you.

So, what's the deal? Why are you stuck? Why aren't you able to move on and do what you need to do? Why are you lying on the floor, letting your fears paralyze you, unable to get things done?

Throughout the years, on my journey to becoming an author and coach, I've been asking myself all of these questions. The process has been slow because, often, I become paralyzed and stuck.

To determine what was keeping me stuck, I did a lot of work on myself. The result is this book.

I want to remind you that this book isn't for everyone.

If you're looking for major life changes and massive success, don't start here.

If you're motivated and can't wait to win at life, Tony Robbins has plenty of books for you.

This isn't the book for people going from stuckiness to greatness. Instead, it's a book that will help you go from stuckiness to momentum.

It's a helping hand, a gentle nudge and a soft whisper to get up off the floor and back onto your chair. It's to help you start that project, continue that project or finish that project. It's to help you move closer to your dreams when the resistance is loud, proud and in your face.

I'm writing to you because I am where you've been – sitting there, wondering why I'm not able to do what I know I'm capable of doing.

If you are tired of the procrastination, tired of the paralysis and tired of not living up to the life you desire, this book is the gentle companion you need.

Let me walk alongside you and help you move forward on this journey.

While I've faced every issue I speak about in this book, the resistance has also struck the many clients I work with and coach. I have worked with them to break through these self-imposed limitations and I've learned from them.

I want to thank them for doing the work, and for working with me to do the work, so they can break free of their resistance, let go of their limitations and live the lives they want.

Cheers to unstuckiness, getting up off the floor and gaining momentum. Cheers to starting, continuing and finishing what you started.

In moving forward,

Vishnu

P.S. If you find this book helpful or need some guidance, please email me at vishnusvirtues@gmail.com. If you enjoyed this book, I would greatly appreciate it if you would leave a review of this book on the Amazon review page.

1. The Inner Resistance

I was down and out.

Divorce was the knockout punch that left me reeling on the mat for years.

Everything I had worked towards came to a crashing halt.

How was I ever going to put my life back together?

I was facing so much pain, confusion and uncertainty.

The law career I had worked on, the marriage that I had started on, the house that I was paying on – it all came to an end. All at the same time.

I moved out of the place we shared, moved my things into my car and moved into someone else's home, where I rented a room.

Soon, I left my job, the career I had worked for and the state where I was living.

Everything I had known ended and there I was, with a carload of everything I'd ever owned.

This was the starting point from where I realized that I couldn't manage the pain I was dealing with. I was so overwhelmed that I almost felt like giving up on life. The pain of heartbreak, the failure of my marriage and the social stigma of divorce were too much to handle.

I found myself in counseling, therapy, coaching and different parts of the world, trying to cope and heal with what had happened throughout the last 10 years of my life.

At rock bottom, I would have to recreate my life and start over.

In the midst of this agony and paralysis, I started writing.

The one thing that my ex had always encouraged me to do was write. She believed that I was a good writer and we had talked about me starting a writing career.

We were probably naïve but we thought that, ultimately, both of us would give up the two professions we were in (law and medicine) and rely on my writing.

Imagine the irony when I started my writing projects only after we had signed the divorce papers.

Writing became the coping and healing mechanism that helped me function.

One of my therapists suggested that I journal to help myself cope with the pain of what I was going through. Little did she know what all the writing and journaling would turn into.

It turned into a blog on which I've written more than a million words. It turned into a publishing business through which I've self-published 10 books. It led to coaching school and, ultimately, coaching others who are going through heartbreak and divorce.

Today, I coach divorcees who are stuck in their past relationships. I also coach others who are stuck in life, not knowing how to break free of the inner resistance holding them back.

This journey has not been easy by any means.

I've had to work against my insecurities, my fears, my doubts and my feelings of not being good enough to do the work I am doing now.

It has been an uphill climb. The thing that has been most present during this journey is inner resistance.

Inner resistance has kept me from achieving things more quickly, from doing what I needed to do and from creating the life I wanted to live. It has kept me on the floor and away from writing. It has kept me hiding and playing small.

I knew my potential and I knew the sky was the limit but the resistance kept showing up like a bully, flattening me.

Resistance has filled each word I've written, each book I've published and each step I've taken on the coaching journey.

Not anything from the outside, either; it has all been clearly from within.

I found it weird that I couldn't achieve my dreams and go after the life I wanted while, around me, people were doing just that.

How do you deal with this inner resistance? Where does it come from? How do you get around it and break free of it? How do you go on to live the life you want?

These are the questions I struggled with and asked myself. These are the questions whose answers I searched for.

These are the questions I answer in this book to help you along your own journey to overcoming, continuing and succeeding.

2. Where Does Resistance Come From?

I can't begin to tell you how many places internal resistance comes from. Oh, actually, let me count the ways because I've experienced them all. I've found reason after reason that has kept me stuck on the floor, preventing me from doing what I know I need to do.

At the most basic level – and a common cause of procrastination and delay – is simply distraction. I get caught up in the world of social media, television (occasionally), emailing or talking to people by phone. Distraction is about doing anything that is more fun, entertaining and easy – and that requires less effort – than doing the thing that needs to get done. Though I love writing and coaching, I sometimes stumble upon something, anything, that will distract me for a few minutes.

A more serious distraction is the past, which has kept me stuck for days or months at a time. This is a heavy burden that comes into my life and pulls me down like quicksand. It feels like being on a boat and wanting to go forward when a heavy anchor is trying to bring you down. You're stuck and you can't move forward even when you feel like you can.

My divorce, my previous failures and every disappointment I experienced while growing up are some of the failures that anchor me down and prevent me from moving forward. I think about what a disappointment and failure I was in my relationship and my marriage. I think about how bad of a professional I was to get out of the legal field. I think about how dumb it was to spend a hundred thousand dollars on a legal education I don't use. I think about not measuring up to people's expectations and hopes for me. I feel bad that I'm not living up to my potential. I could have been doing so well as a successful lawyer when now I am barely making it as a creator and writer.

I fear both success and failure, which holds me back from going forward.

As I'm sitting there on the ground, I'm thinking to myself: What if this writing and coaching stuff worked? What if I actually made it as a famous writer and successful coach? What if all my dreams came true? Well, I wouldn't have time to relax and do life on my own terms. I would have to travel all the time. I wouldn't have my own schedule. Rather, I'd have to cater to everyone else's. I would lose my freedom, my peace of mind and my own schedule!

Also, what if it failed? What if I didn't get what I wanted? What if no one bought my books or hired me as a coach? What if I could never pursue my dreams? What if my work wasn't resonating with people? I would hate to go back to my old life of work and doing the grind. I might have to do things I don't particularly enjoy. I may have to go back to being a lawyer. Gasp! I can't do anything because I'm terrified of failing. I'm terrified of the worst-case scenario.

I look around and see what others are doing. This keeps me frustrated and stuck.

The comparison game is deadly. It's always in my pocket. It's always in my phone.

As a creator, you notice how many followers and fans someone has. Oh, that post they wrote is getting so many likes. That picture they took is simply fantastic. Oh, the life they are living is just unbelievable as they travel the world and eat fancy food. The interviews and podcasts they do are affecting the lives of so many people.

One hundred people read my blog post. Meanwhile, 15,000 people read Leo Babauta's post in the first few hours. My YouTube video gained 100 views. Jay Shetty's video has 50,000. I sold 50 books on this book launch. Jen Sincero has been on the bestselling book list for years on end.

Why even start and why even do anything when all these other creators, writers and influencers are doing so well? Not only are they doing well but they've made all the content. They've said everything that needs to be said on a topic. They have recorded every podcast, spoken every Ted talk, written every book and created every kind of idea out there. How do I even compete? Why do I even participate?

They have created all the content out there, so where do I even start? What if I run out of ideas? I don't have an idea now, so I'm not starting. Or I've experienced resistance when I've had ideas, started on those ideas and then become uncertain about those ideas. Halfway in, I realize the project is boring, doesn't make sense or doesn't seem to be going anywhere. I stay stuck in this place of having started but being unable to finish. The resistance hits hard and prevents me from moving forward.

A big point of resistance for me is worthiness and being seen. Due to some childhood wounds and my upbringing, I've found it difficult to put myself out there because I'm afraid of the responses. I don't want people to talk about me and say bad things about me. I don't want to be visible because I fear criticism, rejection and disappointment from others. They may not agree with me or they may tell me that I'm flat-out wrong.

They may judge or criticize my work which is just as bad as a personal attack on me. No, in fact, attacking my work is worse than attacking me. I don't want people to say bad things about my work. I would rather curl up in a ball, not do any work and just hide, waiting for the day to pass. Each and every day I don't do anything, produce anything, share anything or publish anything is a day that I'm winning against the possible critiques and reviews. Not doing anything is a safe place.

Finally, I fear not being good enough to be the person to talk about these topics that I talk about. I have impostor syndrome and doubt my ability to be the messenger behind my message. Why am I the one who is talking about breakups and divorce in my coaching work? Why am I the expert on this topic? How am I qualified? What do I know? Why should people listen to me?

Each and every day, these thoughts run through my mind. Each and every day, I sit with these thoughts and then get paralyzed, stuck and hesitant to do anything. I roll around on the floor, spending hours on my sleeping bag, looking my fears and obstacles in the face. The minutes, hours and days pass. As time goes by, I feel worse about myself. This is what feeling stuck is like.

While resistance is something you should aim to overcome every day, it can also be an indicator that something deeper isn't right. If you feel like the project or dream you're pursuing is an uphill push, like it's not meant for you or it's not worth continuing, take some time to pause and reflect.

Don't blame resistance if the project or business you're pursuing isn't meant for you. Get deeper into understanding whether the project aligns with your life's principles and values. Try to see if this is something you truly want to do. Does this fulfill your life's purpose? Does this fulfill your life's mission?

Knowing whether the venture you're pursuing is right for you requires self-awareness, self-reflection and self-understanding. It requires that you pay attention to your intuition to determine whether this is the path for you. It requires that you check in with your ego to determine whether you're doing what you're doing because of ego or because of mission.

This book will help you reduce the resistance you experience when you're confronting procrastination and paralysis while doing the thing you're supposed to be doing in the world. If the paralysis and stuckiness come from energy that says this isn't your battle or path, it's time to right the ship and move in a different direction.

Use your experience, wisdom and intuition to continually check in with yourself. Your life's priorities and mission can change over time. Something that you were excited and thrilled about months or years ago may no longer resonate. You may have grown out of this project or idea and be getting ready to move into something else in your life.

Stay true to what is meant for you and pursue it at whatever cost, including moving past the resistance. Stay true to yourself and ditch those things in your life that are not meant for you. If you feel a shift about a life purpose or a change of heart about a life dream, look at the pause with curiosity to determine what is behind the resistance. Is this a case of resisting what you're supposed to be doing or is it a case of redirection and moving on to something else?

Don't push ahead or pass go if the resistance means it's time to head in a different direction. Don't run backwards, canoe upstream or walk up towards an active volcano. Push through if you're on your path to your destiny. Push away if it's not meant for you or not what you truly desire.

3. How Being Stuck Affects Your Life

When you're stuck, you can't achieve what you're capable of achieving. All

your dreams remain stuck. All your potential remains trapped and you're not able to achieve what you know you can.

It's like creating a self-inflicted prison. Your mind and your thoughts are literally preventing you from taking action. Your thoughts send a message to your feelings. Your feelings solidify your belief system. Your belief system prevents you from taking concrete action.

This is how you end up on the floor in your sleeping bag, unable to do the very thing that can move you forward.

In your life, stuckiness is preventing you from starting that business you've wanted to start for years. It can stop you from beginning the project, starting the research, initiating the book or doing the writing. It can prevent you from working on that art project, that music you want to create or that non-profit you want to start. It takes away your momentum, sucks up your initiative and locks you up.

You begin to feel like you're playing small, and playing small makes you feel terrible about yourself. You feel like you're disappointing yourself and letting yourself down. You've done mediocre, hum-drum and playing small. It doesn't feel very good so you get bored and give up on life. You half-heartedly do whatever it is you're doing, waiting for the next paycheck, for the next vacation or maybe for your career to end. It feels like you're just going through the motions of life.

Or even worse, you feel like a zombie when you're not working on the projects you want to work on and going after the life you desire. You feel like you're trapped in someone else's body and just going through the motions. You wonder if this is all there is to life and you constantly regret that you're not living your life's purpose and dreams.

The thing is, you don't have to accept this status quo. You don't have to accept this life that you have taken on by default. You don't have to give up on your projects, art, creativity, business ventures and dreams. Stuckiness is not a permanent place of being. Rather, it's a place of learning and awareness. You figure out whatever it is that's keeping you stuck and then you work around, over or through it.

It's also not something that ever goes away. Those of us who have to keep putting ourselves out there, selling our services or sharing our knowledge or selling our art, know that every time we hit publish, send or ship, we risk rejection or failure. So we continue to feel stuck on a regular basis. We work through those feelings of paralysis and frustration over not going anywhere.

The way to break free is to experiment with and try the different solutions in this book. You know that you're stuck and you likely know the root cause. If you don't, just keep reading. You're going to discover even more reasons why you're stuck and this self-awareness is the key to breaking through your blocks.

There are different solutions for people who are stuck and procrastinating. You have to figure out what will work for you. I have tried and used every solution in this book to create momentum. Ultimately, it's all about a small spark to get you going. You just need a match to light the fire. You might struggle to get started but once you do something for a week or month, there's no stopping you. The sky's the limit.

I've divided this book into three parts. I'll start with solutions to help you get unstuck. These are simple, everyday, practical solutions that will inspire you to get up and get going. In the next part of the book, I'll talk about the bigger blocks that are stopping you from doing what you want. This is the core of your internal resistance – the bigger forces that are keeping you from acting and doing. In these chapters, I'll talk about ways to help you get out of your own way. Finally, we will end with how to create more of the life you want.

All of the steps in this book, again, are not for massive and life-shattering changes. However, if you make small changes every day, you'll see long-term massive changes. I want you to take it at your own pace, work through your own struggles and arrive at the place that you and I know you're capable of reaching.

You can do this.

I want you to know that by virtue of picking up this book, you're committed to doing better. You're committed to breaking free and starting. You're committed to living the life you know is possible for you. Slow and steady will win the day. Let's get started.

Part 1.

Overcoming Internal Resistance

4. A Radical Shift to Less

One of the biggest ways I got stuck in my life was that I had too much going on and I wasn't even sure if that was what I wanted.

See, life happens to you. You don't go about planning life. You get a job, you buy a house, you get a partner, you have kids. All of these things happen and each obligation and commitment takes up a bigger part of your life. One day, you wake up as you are driving to a social dinner with people who are not really your friends and you realize that you hate meeting up with people whom you don't particularly think of as friends!

By no means am I saying that you should bail on all your obligations and commitments but I am asking you to cleanse and rebuild. Get rid of everything you can and then start over. Question everything.

Like my situation, so much is going on in your life that you can't give enough attention to the things that matter. In fact, the overwhelm is making your life harder, messier, busier and fuller but with no meaning.

When your life is full of obligations, busy-ness, endless commitments, no boundaries, other people's priorities and things, things, things, then you will easily feel overwhelmed and stuck. The idea is to stop, contemplate, review, reflect and make a complete cleanse.

In my own life, the divorce helped with this. I didn't have to go out seeking a system or method to cleanse and minimize. Due to the divorce, my relationship shrank by 50% because I lost my partner. I immediately owned 50% fewer things and had 50% less space. I had 50% less family and 50% fewer friends. Then I transitioned out of my legal career, which gave me more time, and found myself as a tenant in someone else's house, which reduced my material possessions by 50%. When I cut out my social activities, all that remained were my yoga classes.

You may not have experienced any traumatic loss that automatically reduced, minimized and halved your life. For you, it's more about making a conscious effort to reduce, minimize, get rid of and live a simpler life.

I'm talking about both the inner and outer lives. I'll briefly touch on the inner life here to give you a taste of what I'm talking about but I want to get more into the outer life. The inner life is essentially what is going on within you. When thoughts, emotions, feelings, beliefs and life principles are clashing, the result is paralysis. When your mental and emotional world is in turmoil, you're not going to feel like doing much. I talk about many of these concepts in Part 2, which focuses on getting out of your own way.

Here, your outer life is your job, your meetings, your commitment and your obligations. It's also your material world. I was able to handle this much more effectively when I hit rock bottom in life. I understand that many of these things might feel impractical and difficult. The idea is to adopt the things that will work for you, not to see how you can't do it. Work with me here!

Look at your life and schedule. Start by noting the things that are no longer serving you. If your job is busy and overwhelming, just become aware of it. If your social schedule, family activities or professional commitments are ruling your life, take stock of that. Notice all the things in your life that are taking up a lot of space and that you're really not feeling. The idea for now is to notice, observe and become intent on making some changes in that area of your life.

When you're caught up with all this overwhelm and busy-ness, it's hard to think straight. So, now that you've called out these areas, what can you do to reduce, cut out or minimize those things? No, you can't cut it all out. You have to drop off your kids at school, and you likely need a full-time job and a house, but what small changes can you make that will increase your happiness and the space available in your life?

What changes can you implement at work that will make it more manageable? What things are you doing outside work every week that feel cumbersome and take up lots of time? What do you need to cut out of your life that you're doing every day? How many hours are you on social media or how many hours do you spend watching television? Become aware of the time sucks – both those that are intentional and those that happen without your paying any attention to them. Create a list of action items to eliminate, cut, reduce or change so that you have more room and breathing space.

Now, I'm not going to give you a whole rundown on minimalism or tell you why you should sell all your stuff and move to Bali. I'm in no way suggesting that. Instead, I want you to reduce the number of physical and material possessions in your life so that you create more space and energy. Things not only occupy your physical space but also add to your mental and emotional space. The more stuff you have, the more attention and thoughts you must give to those things. The more stuff, the more external and internal clutter.

I've found that having more things can feel stuffy and paralyzing. A space has only so much energy. When you have more objects and furniture around you, these things take up more energy in your life. If you want to have more free space so you can breathe easier and not feel cluttered by lots of energy, it's time for a declutter.

Here's an interesting experiment: Get rid of half the things you own, or simply put them in a spare room, closet or storage shed. You'll be surprised at how few things you actually use in the course of a regular day. If you removed half the items from your space, you will notice how much more space you have AND how much you didn't need those things around. You can also have a garage sale to get rid of items you haven't used within the past year or you can sell some of your items online.

The more space – and the less clutter – you have, the lighter and more vibrant the energy will be in the room where you are working. You will feel more inspired, creative and productive when the energy is flowing free and when less stuff is blocking that energy. Minimize, simplify and declutter. Don't block the energy in the room or in your life. The things in your life may be adding to the blocks and energetic resistance that are preventing you from doing the very things you want to do.

I want you to also examine and review the relationships in your life. I understand cutting people out of your life is not easy, practical or always possible but I do want you to know that reducing the amount of time you spend with toxic people – unsupportive people who drain your energy – will take a toll on you. You can't do anything about family and you feel like your hands are tied when it comes to lifelong friendships. I suggest that you look at the relationships to determine which ones are bringing you down and preventing you from doing what's required of you.

Toxic and draining relationships will prevent you from doing the work you're capable of doing. The people around you matter. If they're not the type of people who are inspiring you and moving you to achieve your potential, drastically cut the amount of time you spend around them. I'm talking about the folks on social media, too. If someone is regularly complaining and posting controversial posts that upset you, you have the tools to spend less screen time following their content.

Reduce the time you spend online and in person with people who drain your energy and kill spirit. If you are a garden, the toxic people in your life are the weeds. Productivity, creativity and momentum happen free of toxicity and negativity. Be more aware and conscious of the folks in your life and the energy they bring into it.

Finally, look at your activities and your schedule. What activities are you doing out of obligation and habit? What activities do you actually want to do? What advances your goals and purpose in life? What is a time suck? Review your life to minimize the activities so you're focusing only on those that mean something to you.

Your time is a precious commodity. The more you fill it with people and activities that don't advance your goals, the less of it you'll have for the things that matter. The more meaningless the work you do, the less time you'll have for the meaningful work you really care about. Protect and savor time as you do money.

The purpose of reducing all these various aspects of your life is to create open space that you can fill with the people, activities and objects that do have meaning to you. It is also to create an environment where you are most efficient and productive. Often, we look around at our lives, activities and space and we realize that stagnant energy and an over-busy life surround us. In such circumstances, you may want to do nothing.

By eliminating and reducing all aspects of your life, you become freer to achieve what matters to you. Less busy-ness, fewer social commitments and fewer obligatory events means you get to spend more uninterrupted time achieving your creativity, art and business endeavors.

5. Small Steps to Overwhelm

This is my favorite step to overcoming resistance. In the previous chapter, I spoke quite a bit about clearing up the energy and space for you to live your life.

If you still remain stuck and feel lethargic, consider using the small-step strategy. It's the exact strategy I've used to recreate everything in my life.

If you think that you will wake up and find yourself to be a self-sustaining writer and author, you won't be quite right. If you think you can wake up and be a full-time meditator, athlete or artist, you'll find few examples to show for it.

The biggest tip I can share with you about breaking resistance is also the smallest tip I can share with you. Do not go after the life you want with big leaps and jumps. Do not aim for actions so big that you feel like doing nothing.

If you're on a motivation high, then sure, go big. However, if you're on a motivation low, do the very opposite thing. Take the smallest step you can. Take the tiniest action you can imagine.

It's how this book became my tenth book. It's how this is my third year of meditation. It's how this is my 16th month of regular gym workouts.

Speaking of gym workouts, let me share an experience that got me into the gym. I wanted to be more healthy, but I didn't want to be disciplined or regular about it. One Christmas day, while shopping, I got tired. As I walked miles and miles around the mall, I had an idea.

What if I walked around the mall on a regular basis, to get my walk in and do some exercise? Believe it or not, that is exactly what I did. I used my cell phone to keep time and showed up several times a week to increase the number of steps I walked. Guess what that snowballed into? Regular walking, exercising and getting a little fitter.

As I became fitter, I grew out of mall walking, as it was testing my patience due to the Cinnabon stall and the See's candy store. I thought to myself: Maybe I'll use this seven-day free exercise pass that I got in the mail. Before I knew it, I had signed up for the gym. Every day, I was running on the treadmill for 30 minutes and swimming for 30 minutes. Was this the new me? Was this my exercise regimen and my life? Why, yes it was!

I went from resisting exercise and health to feeling good by spending time in the gym for an hour. This has continued through today. Last month, I was in the gym for 20 out of 30 days, if you can believe it. The gym has been helping me stay motivated by offering free water bottles and T-shirts for regular attendance. Oh, what one will do for free stuff!

This is how all great things happen: one step at a time and one day at a time.

Break down things to the smallest form and the smallest action you can take. You may be feeling uninspired and sitting on the couch, not wanting to take action. What's the smallest and most immediate action you can take? The action that counts is the one you're willing to take. Is it putting on your shoes? Is it walking around the house? Is it walking around the neighborhood?

Is it reading one page, one chapter and then one book? Regardless of the project and endeavor, if you don't feel like getting started on it, then break the activity down to its smallest parts. Start at the very first step of this project or activity. Do just one thing – actually, the very smallest part of that one thing.

I would argue that the smaller the step and the less you do one day, the more motivated you'll be the next day. Don't overdo it and don't go beyond your limits. Don't push yourself to the point that you get frustrated and overwhelmed and therefore lose momentum. Do the small step and incrementally improve upon that small step each and every day.

Focus on consistency much more than on quality or intensity. It's not about how much you do but about simply doing it every day. That's all there is to it. If you feel like you have no time today or like you can't do anything today, do the absolute tiniest thing that will take seconds or minutes of your time. Write 10 words if you're a writer, walk 10 steps if you're on a fitness journey, draft a couple marketing ideas for your business. Move your life forward by seconds and inches every day. Don't run the marathon today.

This idea of doing something every day is what some people call a "habit" but you don't have to call it that. You can call it "daily consistent action" – whatever you want. To keep at it, remind yourself daily about the underlying purpose and the bigger vision you're moving towards. Eliminate the pressure of having to do a lot by going small.

Complete only one or two of these habits a day. Don't work on 20 different things at once. If you do, you'll lose momentum. Commit to doing a couple things but hold yourself accountable to doing them. Do something so small that you can actually complete it. Even if you're stuck and even if you don't feel like doing a thing, make the task in front of you so easy and simple that you can do it.

At first, you can use a couple of tools to help yourself build up this daily practice. You can tell someone you're going to do it and then ask them to keep you accountable. If they are also willing to work on something in their life, you can work on those things together to keep each other accountable.

Another idea is to reward yourself in some way by accomplishing the mini-task you've set for yourself. This can be as simple as what I did when working on my word count towards creating a regular writing practice. On the calendar, I checked off the date when I hit the 500-word or 1,000-word mark. The simple act of crossing things off the calendar made me feel good. Or you can promise yourself some kind of healthy reward if you achieve your daily task for a week or a month. Reward yourself with a gift or ice cream or whatever it is you like in life to help you move the needle on your mini-habit.

Do something small, do it regularly and keep doing it. This is truly the secret to getting unstuck and it's the secret to accomplishing the big things in life. Start small, build momentum and keep going. When others around you are aiming for the fences, you simply aim for the next thing, the next very small thing. While they give up on audacious goals and big dreams, you'll find yourself building momentum and moving forward.

6. Break the Rhythm

As you go about pursuing your dream or life purpose, you might get too comfortable with the stuckiness. You might feel too good about being paralyzed and not doing anything. Inertia and stuckiness feel good because they prevent you from getting out of your comfort zone. When you're not doing anything, you feel safe. There is safety in certainty and the status quo.

When you're on the floor, like I've regularly found myself, a few feet away from the work awaiting me, you just dig into the ground, curl up and relax. I could have stayed like this, and I did, for hours or days. I'd just sit there ruminating on the past, thinking about the present and daydreaming about the future. I traveled in thought while doing no action.

In this chapter, the idea is to get out of these familiar patterns of thinking or doing. How do you break the pattern? Jolt the system. Get up, run around, move your computer, move your books, rearrange your desk, rearrange your bed, rearrange your room, rearrange your furniture. Do whatever it takes to change the pattern.

Do it physically so you break this inner pattern of feeling low, weak and filled with a low emotional vibe. Change your body. Jump up and down. Get out of the place where you are working and go do something. Anything. I've always found that going to the gym or doing some exercise to be immediately helpful in changing my state of being. If you do a little cardio, break out into a dance routine or do some jumping jacks, you will get an immediate boost of different feelings.

You can also watch a motivational video online, listen to the music and feel inspired. You can imagine yourself as being a character from a movie or TV show and role-play that person for a minute. Imagine that you are a TV personality like Ryan Seacrest, a musician like Eminem or a top athlete like Stephen Curry. Personify someone like Andy Warhol or Kanye West for a few minutes. Improvise and put yourself in their shoes for some quick visualization and to change your body chemistry. If you imagine yourself to be a high-powered athlete or world-famous musician, you'll feel an immediate change in your body.

Another physical body trick that I use to change my inner physical state is to feel good. Yes, even if you're feeling deathly, depressed or uninspired, you can fake feeling good for a few minutes. Imagine someone or something that makes you feel good. Close your eyes and let it wash over you. Feel the feelings of being around the people or activities that make you smile. Take yourself back to that trip to Paris. Imagine your nephews or nieces coming to visit. Think of something pleasant and joyful for a couple minutes and it will immediately cause a change of state.

You can jump into a feel-good state or get creative and enter any other state of being. You can get into a state of confidence, a state excitement or a state of adventure. You can get into a state of anticipation like you're about to jump into a ball game. You can get into a state or relief like you're reaching the end of a marathon. You can jump into a state of joy like you won the World Cup or the national title. It may not be happening in your life at this moment but you can jump into these states through your imagination and creativity at any time.

Other than your body, you can change the place where you do your work. Change the environment to get another shot of change and momentum. Maybe the place where you're working is making you feel dull and uninspired. Get out of the house. Get out of the cubicle. Get out of the office. Change the location and maybe even move on to something different or exciting. Go to a fancy hotel and do some work in the lobby. Visit your favorite funky coffee shop. Drive out to the beach or your favorite park. Changing the environment is an automatic way to help you feel more positive.

I'm giving you ideas to try out but what is going to work for you is the idea that you actually attempt. These are not theories or thought exercises that you will ponder and then go back to being stuck. If you want to break out of your habit of being stuck, you'll have to experiment and try new things. You'll have to determine what will help you break free from your patterns of paralysis and help you get moving.

What will give you a shot of motivation? Think, reflect, experiment, act and review. If you try something and it works, do more of it. If it doesn't, try something else. Rinse and repeat this process until you're back on track and moving forward.

7. Inquire Within

When you feel stuck, you may not be asking yourself many questions or you could be asking yourself disempowering questions. You might be asking yourself something like, "Why am I so stuck?" or "Why do I always feel stuck?" or "Why am I the only one who feels so stuck?" These questions aren't the most helpful ones because they remind you of the problem and the fact that you're not able to deal with that problem.

It's helpful to ask why you're stuck so that you can troubleshoot. However, if you keep asking yourself this question and feel bad about the place where you are, it's not helpful. Instead of focusing solely on the problem, ask yourself questions that will lead you to the solution. "What will help me break free of this free place?" "What haven't I tried yet to help me get unstuck?" "What can I try today that will be different?"

Asking yourself these questions is an effective way to get the answer. You can also journal these questions. I asked and journaled these questions to get to the root of what was happening within but the resistance kept showing up every few weeks. This happened throughout the course of a year or so.

Ultimately, I got a couple of coaches and worked with them over the past year. If you're feeling stuck, every answer and solution in this book will help but I had to work with a coach to more quickly uncover what was behind my stuckiness. I worked with a couple of coaches including Audrey Chrisler in California and Kristy Sweetland in New Mexico. Both asked me deep questions to help me get to the crux of what was keeping me stuck and what was preventing me from moving forward.

With Audrey, I figured out that my childhood wounding and shame issues were causing me to play small and avoid being seen. I was afraid of putting myself out there because I feared the negativity and criticism of readers and critics. Although I felt that my life purpose was to write and teach people, I feared backlash, which was related to this childhood wound. Awareness by itself created so much clarity regarding what was missing and what more I needed to do.

I realized that I had created certain contracts with each of my parents and that I had obligations towards them. I came from a home of harsh and critical parents who cared a lot about what other people thought about them. This attitude indirectly ingrained itself in me so that I regarded every action I took through the prism of what other people would think. Audrey and I got to the root of what was keeping me stuck. More importantly, Audrey helped me create new contracts for my inner child and his parents. I had to break the pattern and start anew.

Later, when I fell back into patterns of being stuck, Kristy Sweetland offered guidance, exploration and wisdom. With Kristy, I realized that I was not moving forward because I was stuck in the old world of my non-profit job. I was straddling two worlds. I didn't want to fully give up the past world and move forward because of the fear and uncertainty about making a leap and pursuing what I wanted to do.

Once Kristy helped me see this root issue and I realized that if I couldn't do my work of writing and coaching, I wouldn't be fulfilled, I had no other choice. This simple realization and mindset shift helped me become super productive. That's because I realized that doing the work I'm doing now is the only work I can do. Falling back on my previous work or other work wouldn't be meaningful or fulfilling. When I took the other options off the table, I could fly with this option. Failure or Plan B were no longer choices so I had to double down, go all in and do the work I needed to do.

Am I suggesting that you get a coach? No. Am I suggesting that getting one will help you get unstuck quicker? Exactly! Not only have I received coaching but I also coach people in getting unstuck when their minds, emotions or troubled pasts are holding them back. I'm just mentioning coaching as an effective method or another tool for breaking through the resistance you're facing. Coaching can help you get to the underlying issues faster, have more awareness and develop solutions that will help you achieve the thing you're trying to achieve. I just want you to be aware of coaching as a tool and to realize that it's an option available to you.

Ask yourself questions that will help you figure out how to overcome the feeling of being stuck and what you can do about it instead of living in the place of paralysis. Use questions and self-inquiry to help yourself notice the patterns. Then ask yourself what it will take to break the patterns. In this book, I'm going to give you plenty of ways to attack the problem of being stuck but the best solution is the one that you come up with and that will work for you.

Another inquiry you can make if you're feeling stuck is to ask this "stuckiness" energy to speak to you. Get curious about this energy and try to understand how it feels, how heavy it is, where it's located in your body and how it radiates throughout your body. You can try to learn, understand and get familiar with this energy for the sake of overcoming or healing it.

Try to identify where this energy is in your body and what the energy feels like. Then ask this energy of stuck feelings if it has a message for you. Inquire within your body to find out what it has to say. Yes, imagine it can speak. What is it saying to you? What does it need you to know? What does it need you to understand? What does it need you to do? What does it need so that it can subside and allow you to work again?

This imaginative and communicative exercise is powerful and can work if you give it a try. Yes, you're asking yourself, and yes, you're in your own mind. However, when you ask yourself questions, your mind gives you answers. You learn powerful answers from yourself. You know the answers and you know the points of paralysis. Your intuition is your deepest and wisest guide.

Use your ability to ask questions, your ability to explore answers within and your ability to listen to yourself as tools to help you figure out where the stuck energy is coming from and what you can do about it. Use the help of powerful questions for yourself, journaling, inquiry and even coaches to get at what's underlying the resistance. You can learn more about Kristy at www.coachingtocomealive.com and about Audrey at www.audreychrislercoaching.com.

You can also check out my own offerings and coaching at the end of this book.

8. Know How You Work

A way to break paralysis and overwhelm is to get really clear about yourself and how you work, in the sense of what inspires you to get started or do work. In my case, I am very averse to having a schedule of any kind. I prefer the model of the chaotic artist. I cannot calendar things, use to-do lists or have a plan on how to get things done because it would really impinge on my freedom. If I had to work by a rigid schedule or according to a rigid time frame, I would not be at my best.

Yet, even though I knew this about myself, I wasn't getting things done. For most of the day, I wouldn't do anything because I didn't have much to do. When you're going about things by what seems like the seat of your pants and attacking what seem like random projects from the outside, it's simply easier to do nothing. It wasn't working and I wasn't getting anywhere so I had to experiment and start making some changes.

I asked myself and experimented with what would work when it came to a schedule and organizing my work. Not having any set time, schedule or commitment wasn't working, so what was the next-best alternative? If you told me that I had to accomplish 10 tasks a day within eight hours, I simply couldn't do it. So, I had to compromise. I found this strategy to work better for me. I set three to-do items for each day, each week and each month. This was a big thing for me because while these activities made me feel restricted and confined, they also gave me some order and some kind of structure.

I know that, as a creative, I likely work better without any restrictions or limitations. However, having some expectations and order for the day helped me get moving a little more and break out of the absolute freedom I had to not accomplish a thing. I found this out only because I tried something that was different from how I regularly worked.

We all work and perform differently. Some of us like schedules and structures. The rest of us thrive in complete chaos and freedom. I'm among the latter. How about you? Whichever type of person you are, switch it up. If you're someone who follows calendars, schedules and tight routines, break free of it for some time. Don't be so rigid with the schedule you've created for yourself. If you're someone like me and you can't fathom the thought of scheduling something, then switch it up. Create two or three to-do items for the day and indicate the times when you're going to do them.

In addition to changing things up for your schedule, change things up in terms of when you do work. When is your peak state of performance and achievement? From a young age, I've known that I work best in the early mornings. However, of late, when I was facing resistance, I didn't do the work that mattered until after dinner. I started working at 7 pm or so, went late and found that this change in time gave me a boost of energy. If you're a morning person, try the afternoons or evenings. If you're a night owl, try a different time of day to break the pattern. Again, switch it up and experiment.

If you find it hard to start on things because you don't know what to do, take a couple minutes at the beginning or the end of the day to plan. You need less than two minutes to write what you must accomplish for the day or what you must accomplish for the next day. Do some calendaring and scheduling so that when you sit down to work, you know exactly what you need to do. We fidget as we hem and haw, we play with our phones when we don't have an action plan to get us going. Determine whether having a pre-planned list of activities gives you some clarity before you start the day and have an action plan to get yourself going.

Another thing to know is whether you prefer to start with the trivial and get that out of the way first or if you like to start with the important and most challenging work. Knowing this about yourself will help you start with your strength. Some people like to build momentum by starting with the smallest tasks and responsibilities, working towards the most important one. Others may prefer to start with the work that they find most difficult and unpleasant. If they can get that task out of the way, they can enjoy themselves and do the more meaningless tasks that don't require their full attention or focus.

Do you work in short increments or long increments? Do you work best in 30-minute spurts or hour-long spurts? Do you work best with music on or off? In a noisy atmosphere or in a quiet atmosphere? At work at your desk or at the coffee shop? With lots of light and in a bright room or with dim lights and in a darker room? With cool air and open windows or in a room with the air-conditioning blasting and all the windows closed?

Also, be mindful and become more aware of the activities and projects that you enjoy doing and that invigorate you. Which activities naturally and intrinsically motivate you and which do you face with a lot of resistance? If you're facing a lot of resistance overall, which activities or projects do you resist less? Which ones can you start on quicker and which ones do you procrastinate on for hours?

More than likely, there is something deeper about certain projects that causes you to take hours getting started on them. We'll come back to that later in this book. If you are regularly avoiding certain projects, dig a little more into that and see what's really going on there.

Either way, it's good to become familiar with the work you do quickly and the work that causes you to stay stuck for longer periods of time. Behind the resistance are clues and messages that you must uncover but the first step is awareness and acknowledgment of the fact that you are resisting. You can then start trying to figure out why the resistance existence and how you can deal with it.

You may not believe that all of the little things in this chapter matter. However, we are trying to minimize the number of things that prevent you from starting and taking action. Different people respond differently to sounds, temperature, light, etc. If any of these factors are contributing to your ability to start or keep working, then address them.

Experiment, see what works and change things if they are not working for you. Maybe these trivial things are not preventing you from starting. However, if they are, you must get them out of the way so that you can focus on the more important things.

9. Stop Resisting Resistance

Not being where you want to be in life can lead to severe internal resistance. Not liking your situation or your place in life can cause paralysis. You might feel that you need to be farther along on your journey, be more successful than you currently are or have achieved more than you already have.

You may feel that life is unfair and that others are doing much better or are more successful than you are. You may find more successful artists, writers, authors, entrepreneurs or businesspeople around you. Whatever your field is, you notice that others are doing better in it, causing you to procrastinate even more. Success feels elusive and far away.

Your frustration over not starting is also keeping you from starting. You're angry at yourself and unhappy that you're resisting the very thing you want to be doing. You don't believe you should have any resistance in this area. You're stuck and reading books like this to figure out how to overcome the feeling of inner paralysis.

Let's start with acceptance of where you are. Stop resisting resistance. It is what it is. Imagine you are the owner of a hotel and resistance shows up at the door. Instead of shutting the door and locking out resistance, welcome it in. Get acquainted with resistance, have a cup of coffee with resistance and make an effort to really get to know resistance. Be willing to fully accept and embrace resistance and make it part of the family.

No need to push it out. No need to fight it. No need to run away from it. No need to get angry or upset at it. It is what it is. You're doing you and you're allowing resistance to be within you. The idea isn't to push out resistance as much as it is to let it be. You want to take away resistance's power over you. You want to reduce the volume of the resistance in your psyche. Resistance can be there but if you don't feed it with your attention and if it isn't taking over your life, it's a win/win.

Acceptance is allowing the resistance to be. It's honoring the resistance and recognizing that there is a place for it. Remind yourself that sometimes resistance is necessary to keep you away from places where you shouldn't be going. Resistance, if not fear or overwhelm, can be your intuition speaking to you, telling you to not do something or that engaging in a particular project isn't your journey. Resistance can stay but it doesn't require all your time and attention. It doesn't require you to feel bad about it or to have any particularly strong feelings towards it.

Stop avoiding feeling resistance. An alternative space to think about resistance is to focus on what is going right and what you can be thankful for in your life. Instead of focusing on your inability to do something, why not spend time being thankful for the things you have been able to achieve?

In my own case, since starting a writing and coaching career, I haven't grown or become as successful as I would have liked. I've had to go back to part-time and full-time work over the years, and this was a point of frustration. I was not doing what I wanted to be doing all the time. I was feeling resistance in continuing to do the thing I had started.

Of course, once I took a step back, I realized how incredibly fortunate and thankful I was for all the opportunities in front of me. If I shifted focus, I could look at the number of lives I had helped through either my coaching or my books. I thought about all the people who write to me, thanking me for my words and for sharing my experiences.

I also became aware of my ability to do work for a non-profit whose mission I believe in and that pays me well while giving me plenty of time to work on my writing and coaching business. I am thankful for the journey of moving on from divorce and getting to a place where I can plan my life and live it on purpose. If I focus on these things instead of on the reasons why I'm stuck, my entire outlook changes.

Similarly, I want you to think about the project or business you have started. Think about how far you've come on that. Reflect on the courage and initiative it took to get something going. Not only are you doing what others aren't, but you're doing it with courage and enthusiasm. What has gone right? How far have you come? Who has helped you along the way? What are your achievements and accomplishments?

As far as the resistance at hand, you can focus on what you haven't done or you can shift your attention to what you have done. This is less readily noticeable to you because your mind focuses on what you aren't doing. You know how they say that if you think of a blue car and look around you, you'll notice many blue cars while not noticing any other color? What if you noticed the things you were thankful for and that you were actively working on instead of the things you weren't?

Take a moment to reflect on what has been going right. Whatever project you're stuck in, brainstorm five observations about it that you are thankful for. What things about this work make you grateful? To do this actively, carry 10-20 pennies (or similar coins) with you throughout the day. Every time you feel grateful for something, drop a coin into a jar or a cup. By the end of the day, you should have dropped all 20 coins. I myself move the pennies from one side pant pocket to the other side pant pocket as a regular daily practice.

I know this sounds weird but it actively helps me look for gratitude in my everyday life. The more you enter the space of gratitude, the less likely you are to remain stuck. The gratitude energy inspires you and encourages you to work and move forward. The more you can cultivate gratitude in your life, the more productive you will be and the more all aspects of your life will improve. Going through the day being thankful helps attract more positivity and goodness into your life.

Another way to go about thankfulness is to be thankful for the future. No, you haven't gotten what you've wanted yet but, yes, you can still be thankful for it. Imagine having achieved whatever you're going after. Feel what that feels like. Cultivate feelings of gratitude and thankfulness that you will have later but feel them now.

One last way to feel contentment and appreciation is to take the focus off yourself for a minute. How often are you thinking about yourself, what you have to gain and what you have to do? How often do you focus on your priorities, goals and desires?

We are humans, after all, so it's natural that we put ourselves first. However, we don't have to be self-focused at all times. To break your paralysis, turn your focus onto the people, customers, clients or patrons whom your work is serving. Think about how they benefit from your work. How is the work going to motivate, inspire, help or provide a service to them? How will they benefit and how will they feel if you complete what it is you need to complete?

Or you can just go all in on service. A feel-good way to break the stuck energy is to take a break from the work you're doing and, instead, do something nice for someone else. You can do something for your spouse, kids, family or friends. Or you can take it up a notch and do some volunteer work or service in the community. You can help a neighbor or anyone who needs assistance. Just look around and see what you can do. Offer to pick up someone from the airport, housesit, clean a yard, wash a car or visit an elderly neighbor.

There are no limits to kindness and helping others. The best part is that when you help others, you feel good and in high spirits. This should give you additional boost, a changed perspective and a slight high when you come back to the work you must do. A slight focus away from yourself and onto others can give you the tiniest bit of momentum to further the project you're working on.

If you've been feeling stuck for days or weeks, help someone. The feelings of productivity or the feel-good vibes of helping someone will carry over to the work you're doing. You can get quite a feel-good high by giving back and helping people. It will help you get out of your thoughts, struggles and inertia.

Part 2.

Get Out of Your Own Way

10. Thought Clarity

I've always found it fascinating that the difference between two people lies in what is happening inside of them and flowing from their minds. The big differences between the people who are getting things done and succeeding in this world are their thoughts and mental patterns. I want to give you a powerful example of something in my own life that allowed me to simply change my thoughts. It turned everything around.

It was a speech I gave in high school when I ran for student council. I was in my junior year and I was running for senior class president. I gave a terrible speech in front of my classmates. I spoke fast, practically running through the speech, and people gave me looks that seemed to be saying, "What the heck are you talking about?" It was a disaster. Yet with four candidates running, I somehow eked out a win against three popular girls and went on to serve as the senior class president.

This isn't a story about victory so much as it is a story about my public speaking defeat. My speech was so bad that I continued to think about what a terrible job I had done. This led me to Toastmasters when I started college. Now, for some odd reason, I joined this organization even though college students typically don't get involved in an organization like this. I participated in this organization all throughout undergraduate school until I became so confident in my public speaking skills that I ended up applying to, attending and graduating from law school, ultimately becoming a lawyer who defended cases in a courtroom.

Yes, me! The kid who couldn't give a speech to his classmates in an auditorium went on to deliver persuasive speeches to juries, asking them to find his client innocent. Do you know how much thought work went into this project of going from "I'm terrible at public speaking" and "I'm a failure at speaking" to success and confidence in speaking to crowds? The primary difference that I noticed, more than the practice, was the thoughts I had about giving a speech. I went from thinking I was terrible at it and not a good speaker to thinking I was a competent and effective speaker.

The biggest obstacle between you and what you want is what's in your head. Like most things, you completely ignore or overlook the very thing that's right in front of you or within you. The most impact you can have in terms of helping yourself get unstuck is thought work. However, you likely believe that you don't have time to do this. With assignments and projects due, who has time to think about their thoughts? However, thoughts are the things that are ruling your life. They are the root of the feelings, beliefs and actions you take. If the very thing that is keeping you stuck is in your head, isn't it time to examine it?

Let's discuss some ideas about the mind and how thoughts work. Start with this premise. Instead of "Just because I think it, it must be true," take the following approach: "The fact that I'm thinking it doesn't mean it's true." Do not believe this culprit, robber and inner self-sabotager.

I'm going to use some legal metaphors to help make the case to you. (Sorry for all the bad puns in the process.) The fact that your mind comes up with something does not make that thing true. Your mind is unwieldy and distracted. It has no self-control. It's like a wild animal that that has never been trained. Would you hang out with a wild boar in the woods? Ummm...no. You would run for your life!

Start with the premise that whatever your mind is thinking isn't true and you're going to become a more independent judge of the thoughts in your mind. Instead of believing everything hook, line and sinker, you are going to start taking note and evaluating the contents of your thoughts to determine how true they are. The fact that it's a thought doesn't make it true and doesn't mean you have to act on it. You're going to become an independent, objective evaluator of everything that goes through your mind.

Before you get to play judge, though, I'm asking you to play cop. Start this process by deciding to watch and observe your thoughts. Many of us find it hard to watch our own minds. You may have a hard time watching something that is happening within you. You may be too close to your own thoughts to see what they're doing in your mind.

I am asking you to become the police officer of your mind in terms of observation. Just like a police officer is on the lookout for robbers, thieves and bad guys, you'll be on the lookout for negativity, self-sabotage and self-criticism. Be a vigilant police officer, as the crime is happening literally under your nose (or above your nose, in your mind!). Ferret out the negativity and self-critical thoughts that fill your mind. Be prepared to issue a citation and give your thoughts a ticket.

How do you pick up on these thoughts? The idea is to speak them out and observe what you say about things when you say them to other people. Or you could write down your thoughts in a diary or journal format. If you write things out, you can clearly see, in front of your eyes, how you're thinking about something that is going on in your life.

If you have some kind of daily writing practice in which you talk about your day and what you are thinking about, you'll start becoming more observant of the thoughts floating through your mind. It is possible to watch your thoughts if you learn to slow down your mind. That's why practices like meditation are helpful because they help you focus on your breath while you watch your thoughts float by. You slow down to realize that you are not your thoughts. Thought bubbles are floating across your mind. You and your thoughts are two different entities.

As you become the observer and even judge of your thoughts, see which ones are on repeat, which ones are the loudest and which ones create the biggest emotional reactions in you. The thoughts that should stand out and that you should pay attention to are those that say things like you're not good enough, you're not smart enough, you're not able enough or you're not knowledgeable enough to do the things you want to do in life. These are the same thoughts that made me think I wasn't a good public speaker and was a failure at speaking to the public. Catch these thoughts, which will be speaking to you loudly and clearly. There probably aren't many of them. Your most prevalent thoughts repeat themselves a lot and come in many forms.

Not only observe them but become an active searcher for those negative thoughts. Once you have a clear idea of what your self-sabotaging thoughts are, treat the situation like a treasure hunt. Give yourself a point for every time a negative thought pops into your brain. Turn it into a game in which you're searching for these prevalent self-sabotaging thoughts.

Proactively search for these thoughts on replay and celebrate in some way when you pick up on them. Yes, I'm actually asking you to focus on the negative thoughts. However, don't focus on believing them; focus on becoming aware of them when they pop up in your mind. "There you are again…," "There it is…," "Found you…" It's a game of hide and seek in which sneaky thoughts hide behind rational-sounding ideas but are really full of negativity about your ability to achieve what you want in life.

Now that you have become a hunter of negative thoughts, you're more likely to notice them when they come up. As they do, you're going to rebut them like a lawyer would. You are going to make the case to these negative thoughts as to why they aren't true. You're going to provide rational reasons, objective arguments and passionate pleas about why they are dead-wrong. You are going to out-think, out-argue and out-persuade these negative thoughts. You're going to tell these thoughts that they may be many and frequent but you are going to take away their power. You are going to figure out what's wrong with them, discover how to undermine them and find flaws in their arguments.

If your thoughts say that you're not good at something, you're going to come up with a list of reasons why you are good at it. If your thoughts say that you'll never get there, you're going to show your thoughts why you're on track. If your thoughts make you believe you're not smart enough, talented enough or worthy enough, you're going to come up with a list of items to combat that. Rebutting and countering thoughts will become part of your daily mental and spiritual practice. You're in a courtroom and you get to play judge to determine what thoughts are worth your time. You're also going to play lawyer to decide which thoughts you should out-argue and undermine.

As you rebut negative thoughts, you can use affirmations or positive thoughts to replace them. Come up with a list of thoughts that you'll have handy when the negative ones pop up. Because you've already done the thought work and have proven disempowering thoughts to be wrong, you'll be ready with one-liners, talking points and sound bites, prepared to combat the onslaught of negativity. "There is nothing wrong with you." "You have plenty of talents." "You were meant to do this." "You have all the skills you need." "You are a work in progress." "You are qualified."

As you have a steady stream of thoughts in your back pocket to combat the negativity, be prepared to do this over a period of time. Regard this exercise as a process of thought change and reprogramming. The other negative program has been running by default for so long, you never even noticed it. It was a default program that you never took out to examine and it has been in place for many years of your life.

What I'm asking you to do is relatively new for you. If you were a thought-believer and never called on your inner police to investigate your mind, your inner judge to evaluate the thoughts and your inner lawyer to argue against the negative one, this entire process will be new to you. The process is observing, evaluating and taking away the power that those thoughts have over you. You don't have to use the methods or ideas here; you're welcome to adopt a different system that works for you. You're dealing with a common and street-savvy pick-pocketer (your mind), but your knowledge and abilities will put your mind in check.

Because it's a new process, it's going to take time, energy and effort, yet it's well worth it because your mind, without question, is the biggest blocker preventing you from getting things done. It's like a bunch of wild animals in the zoo that distract, play and trip you up so you're not able to focus and do the things you want to do. This will take time but, again, it'll be well worth your time.

You no longer have to let your thoughts hold you prisoner. You're going to become the police, judge and lawyer of your thoughts. You are taking away the power from unruly and wild street thieves and taking back your own power to create the thoughts you want, affirm positivity and help your mind get in sync with the life you desire.

11. Intentional Feelings

Your thoughts affect the quality of your life, but, on a more powerful level, they also affect your feelings. Your thoughts speak through your feelings, which makes your thoughts doubly powerful. When your thoughts tell you something that's unhelpful or negative, your feelings get in the way and make it seem as though your thought is, in fact, true. Your thoughts are the cause, while your feelings are the effects of those thoughts. You feel overwhelm, inadequate, like a failure, sad, stuck because of the thoughts that your mind generates.

Later, I will talk more about one of the life-changing incidents in my life. However, I want to mention one thing about my life post-divorce. It was the time when I felt the worst about myself. The divorce was the action that created many negative thoughts. I'm not good enough. I'm a failure. My ex – the person who was the other member of my most intimate relationship – dislikes me. I had a string of thoughts about myself that then made me feel terrible. My thoughts generated feelings of shame, rejection, pain, guilt, loss and grief. I wore these feelings for way too long. The thoughts created the feelings and the feelings were the anchor that tried to pull me farther into the deep sea of suffering.

While thoughts generate hurtful emotions, it's those emotions that drown us. They are heavy, they are usually toxic and they typically try to prevent us from getting anything done. Thus, the first step in dealing with emotions is to realize where they come from. Most people accept feelings as they are and think they can't do anything about them. I think the first idea is simply to be aware that feelings don't come out of thin air. Rather, they come from your thoughts. You generate those thoughts, and feelings are the effect of those thoughts. If you want to change how you feel, you have the power to make that change.

Learn how to see your feelings as a guide to your life. You usually feel and experience emotions without watching or observing them. You and the emotions you feel are one and the same. What if you became a little more aware of them? What if you labeled them as they came up? What if you noticed and paid attention to how you're feeling? What if you noticed the thoughts that are generating those emotions?

Start thinking of your emotions as guides. Use them to navigate the world and the tasks in front of you. If you're having particularly strong feelings against doing something, try to figure out what about that thing is unpleasant or why you're resisting it. Use your emotions as detectors to determine how you feel about a particular task or project. Get feedback from your emotions and analyze them. Know the message they're giving you.

Once you experience emotions and have identified their root, focus on changing the underlying thoughts that we spoke about in the previous chapter. Change your thoughts and change your emotions around them. Also, to help yourself change the emotion, try changing the meaning of something happening to you.

For example, let's say you're facing obstacle after obstacle in trying to publish a blog post today. You could be thinking that the world is out to get you and you're destined to fail. This could make you feel overwhelmed, out of control and like a failure. If you sat back a minute and changed the meaning, you would change the feelings. You could, for example, think that you're learning resiliency in overcoming the technical difficulties of posting a blog post. You could think that you're getting better at the craft of posting blog posts. You could be thinking that successful bloggers and writers overcome whatever is in their way. If you changed the meaning of the problem, you'd feel much better about what you're experiencing.

When you're in a bad mood or feeling low for long periods of time, thereby preventing yourself from starting or doing anything, go ahead and consciously change those feelings. Just practice feeling good, even if you're in the throes of sadness or unhappiness. Try on new feelings for a bit, just to see the contrast. Generate thoughts in your mind that would help you feel good in the moment. As you complete this exercise, notice that you have the power to proactively and consciously change the feelings and emotions in your life.

Another practice I like is to feel good for a few minutes every day. We get used to feeling bad every day but what if you intentionally and purposefully entered a state of feeling good? The idea here is to think about things that make you happy or things that you're grateful for. Feel some happiness, gratitude or love from your heart center and let it spread throughout your body. Send the vibration out from within you to around you.

Even if you're going through some down hours or days, a couple of these practices can help you break out of the "feelings rut." You don't have to remain stuck in the emotions you're feeling and you don't have to let them overwhelm you to the point that you experience paralysis. If you're in that state, try these small exercises. Feel good and know that you can change your feelings. Generate love and gratitude daily to know that you can proactively cultivate positive feelings.

If you can't do the thought work to change your feelings, then try physical exercise or activity. Usually, your spiraling thoughts become so heavy, they paralyze you. The way to break out of your thought pattern and do something more productive is to get physical. Instead of lying in bed or on the floor, get up and out of the house. Break free of the paralysis of feeling bad by boosting your heart rate. Do something, anything, that will get you breathing and your heart pumping to break the cycle of negative feelings.

One last technique is to see yourself experiencing more positive feelings. In your mind's eye, see yourself feeling good and positive. Use the power of visualization to envision yourself feeling better about things and getting things done.

I don't want to discount the power of feelings and emotions in your life, nor do I want to imply that strong negative feelings are always changeable and curable. Sometimes, negative emotions are so strong and overwhelming, you can't do anything about them. That may be the time to get professional help or to speak to someone about the heaviness of those emotions.

However, if you're experiencing negative emotions only sporadically, and if this is preventing you from getting started or progressing on your work, know that you have some tools to change those emotions. Change the thoughts you're experiencing or change the meaning of the underlying event. Proactively change your thoughts and try feeling good for parts of the day. Visualize and see yourself feeling good. Get physical exercise and get active to change your emotional state.

You don't have to let your feelings and emotions hold you captive. There are ways to transform and change your emotions to get them on your side so you can move forward and get things done.

12. Your Beliefs or Your Barriers

Your life is a series of beliefs that shape your future. Thoughts, feelings, previous experiences and perspectives shape your beliefs. If you had bad business partners, you'll see business partnerships one way. If an audience didn't appreciate your art, you'll believe that no one is into your art. If someone stole or cheated you before, you'll tend to view people a certain way.

One interaction, one experience, one past bad situation can inflict a lot of damage to your belief system. In turn, your belief system has a way of skewing your outlook and actions. Belief systems are overwhelming and life-altering; they prevent you from even starting. If you believe you aren't good, you don't have the experience, you aren't worthy or you won't succeed, those beliefs will have a lot of impact on the actions you take.

I coach people in both mindset and relationships, so I see a lot of limiting beliefs. Limiting and disempowering belief systems are even more prevalent and deep-rooted than excuses. People come up with excuses because they want to avoid doing something. They come up with practical reasons for why they can't do something or they devise false obstacles that prevent them from dealing with something.

Beliefs are a whole different level. Powerful beliefs will stop you from starting, or will even make you believe that you can't possibly do the thing you want to do. They will prevent you from even considering the notion that you can do it or that you can succeed in doing whatever it is you want to do. Common beliefs are that you're not capable enough or you don't have enough experience or you don't know what you're doing yet or you don't have enough money to start.

You take one perspective and hold onto it like it's the truth. People believe you can't make money from art. People believe you can't quit a 9-5 job and succeed as a freelancer. People believe you need lots of capital to start a business. People believe you need lots of degrees or many more courses to do the thing you want to do. The practical effects of beliefs are that they prevent you from starting.

Your thoughts ultimately shape your beliefs. Over a period of time, well-rehearsed and well-practiced thoughts turn into beliefs. Childhood messages, interactions and experiences turn into strong beliefs. If your parents had a particular religious or political view of the world, you likely adopted those beliefs in your own life. Your culture or society may dictate beliefs about jobs you can enter, what you can do, whom you can marry and by what age you need to have a family.

Similar to thought rebuttal, you must examine every belief that comes up. The biggest breakthrough about beliefs is realizing that you even have a limiting one. If you're not able to start, think about all the reasons why. What is it about this project or venture that is preventing you from starting? Is it because you doubt your ability to do this? Is it because you feel like the task is too mundane and beneath you? Is it because you don't feel like you can do this at your age?

Whatever the underlying beliefs are, your work is to question them and cast doubt on them. When you have clearly identified a belief, look for the opposite idea of that belief. Entertain and introduce ideas that oppose those beliefs. If you think you're too old to start, look for even one person who started at your age. If you think you're not smart enough, look at someone who started with fewer qualifications than you have. If you don't believe you're worthy enough or experienced enough or capable enough, look at one other person whom you know more about.

One belief I have had is that you cannot earn a living doing what you enjoy doing. I believed the only way to earn a living was to be a professional because my parents had drummed this belief into me when I was a kid. So, for a few years, I was timid and hid my content from people because I didn't take my writing and personal development work seriously. 'This can't be a real profession. It's more like a hobby,' I thought.

Of course, I started doing more writing and earning money from books and coaching. Consequently, I realized that my belief was not true. I then changed my thought patterns and consciously tried to affirm thoughts that this was possible. I watched people who were doing it. I took coaching courses and spoke to other people who were doing this. I watched and learned and kept my mind open to a set of beliefs that opposed the one I was carrying around. As I write this book, I am in the middle of my shift, transitioning from an employer to doing more coaching and writing.

The formula is the same for you. Once you have discovered a belief that is holding you back, your work is to actively change it. You must affirm the opposite of the belief and repeat that thought to yourself as often as possible. To create a new belief, you must cultivate a new set of feelings and emotions. If you believed that new belief, what thoughts and feelings would you have about it? Think those thoughts and feel those feelings. Regularly! Be intentional and conscious about it.

As you change the way you feel about a particular belief on the inside, take courageous action that is the opposite of the previous belief. If I didn't believe that people would read my writing, I had to take a step and publish it. If I believed that I wasn't an author, I had to take the step of self-publishing a book. If I didn't believe that I was an expert on a topic, I had to get out there and speak about it on a podcast or video. If I didn't believe that I was a competent public speaker, I had to join Toastmasters, practice giving speeches weekly, go to law school, continue improving and finally represent clients in a courtroom.

I've practiced changing beliefs over and over in my life. As I said, it all starts with the realization that what's holding you back are your beliefs – not anything else. It's a realization that this inner voice you have developed over your life stems from fear-based learnings that are not necessarily true. The way you've operated by default doesn't have to be the way you live now. You can change the script by changing the thoughts, feelings and actions. Once you change your belief, you change your life. Your own perspective and small-thinking no longer limit you. You are open to doing what you're capable of and what you desire. Small beliefs keep you small. Breaking out of them will help you fully embrace what you're able to achieve.

I want to give you an idea of how beliefs have shaped your life in certain ways. A very common belief that we all hold onto is that we will graduate from high school. We do. Some people go to college because they believe they need to do so, as it's what their families expect them to do. We all believe that we are going to live a long life, and a vast majority of us do, as lifespans have continued to increase over the years. You believe you're going to live long, so you live long. There are many of these underlying beliefs that work in our favor…so why not use other beliefs in our favor as well? Why not believe that you're going to be successful and impactful, that you'll achieve your vision for the world?

One tool you can use to shape and change your belief system is something I call "active envisioning." One of my law school professors taught me this technique and it's one of the most powerful techniques I've learned. You may not be able to change your thoughts or beliefs today because of the circumstances around you. You look outwards and see your lack of progress, your lack of success and your failures. You see how far you haven't gotten and what you haven't started yet. You can't see the end goal or the victory.

Cue my law professor, Dennis Saccuzzo, who is an eccentric yet brilliant bar passage professor and, I believe, the sole reason why I passed the California bar exam to become a lawyer – and on my first try. I'm not kidding here; after our bar prep classes, he made us lie on the floor and close our eyes. He made us go to a deep place of relaxation and had us envision what it would feel like to pass the bar exam. He made us look not only at the possibility of passing the bar exam but at everything from getting the mail to opening the letter to jumping with joy knowing that we had passed the exam.

He got us into this habit on a regular basis and it worked for me. As I mentioned, I passed the bar exam on my first try. I noticed that he conditioned us into a state of success by not only visually imagining what we wanted but by getting into a complete physical state of passing the exam and being practicing lawyers. He made us see what was possible and feel the feeling of having achieved what we saw in our mind's eye.

You can do this if you're facing resistance in any area. If you don't see yourself completing something, or don't see the finish line, get into a state of relaxation. Count down from 10 to 1 and take deep breaths. As you do this, wear comfortable clothing and be in a comfortable place. Now start imagining what it would look like to achieve or get the thing you wanted. Look at that picture with its visual clues, its colors, its temperature, the brightness of the surroundings. Also, start feeling the feelings of having achieved it. How would you react, act, walk, feel and move once you achieve this? What song would you play in the background? How would you describe the feelings and vibrations internally?

You can create this future place in your mind to help you know where you're going. When the mundaneness or challenges of daily activity come up or when you face the obstacles that accompany your creative work or business, it's helpful to transport yourself to this future place to remind yourself of what you're working towards. You can capture this place with a symbol, object or photo that you put up near your workstation or desk. Near where I write and coach people, I have pictures of calm, peaceful and spiritual places where I can live. I have a visual image in my mind but magazine cut-outs on the wall serve as a reminder of what I'm moving towards.

13. Face Your Fears

If not for my fears, I would be so much further along with my online ventures, writing and coaching practicing. My biggest fear this entire time has been what people will think of me. What will people think of me when they see my writing online? What will they think of me if they see something controversial? What will they think of me if I say something they don't agree with or something that offends them?

It was so hard to be myself and market my writing when I thought people would say terrible things about me, reject me or banish me from their lives. I thought they wouldn't talk to me or want to talk to me. I have since realized that my inner circle of friends and family are not my target audience. They are not the ones who are buying my books or hiring me for coaching. Also, they hardly have time to read anything I write or keep up with my work.

The fears that I had in my mind and that prolonged my work for a long time were mostly delusional and non-existent. We think up these thoughts that do not stem from reality; our minds love being able to scare us. It is a creative theater of dramatic arts that brings out all of our worst possible scenarios and all of the unrealistic possibilities. Most of your doubts and fears are not realistic. I'm going to suggest some ways to tackle your fears and clear them from your path.

To start, simply understanding what's at the root of your fear will help you eliminate the power of that fear. You may fear starting because you'll fail. You may fear starting again because you've tried it before and it didn't work. You may fear something because you don't know how it's going to turn out. You may fear taking this action because people will laugh at you. Simply getting clear on the reason you're fearing something will help you reduce the power of the fear. Take a minute to really understand, name, acknowledge, call out and identify the fear. When you speak it out or write it out, you'll have a startling moment: "Oh, this is what I'm afraid of?" It won't be as scary as your mind makes it out to be.

After you've identified your fears, take them to an extreme. As you know, most fears don't actually materialize. You think about something over and over again but, more than likely, your worst fears have never materialized. This technique involves taking your fear and going with it. Let's say you fear starting a project because you'll lose money on it. You don't want to invest in a camera, let's say, because it will put you out a couple thousand dollars. Imagine losing that $2000. Then, imagine not being able to pay your credit card bill. Imagine having to file bankruptcy. Imagine losing the place where you live. Imagine moving in with relatives. Keep going until you reach a situation that's as drastic as you can make it.

As you complete this exercise, you'll realize that your fears are more and more outlandish. You'll realize that the very thing you fear is unlikely, as are the worst-case scenarios. I want you to see how preposterous the entire sequence of events is in your mind. Once you see how things play out to the extreme, and as you imagine your absolute worst fear materializing, you'll realize two things: It likely will never materialize and, even better, if it did, it's okay. You're going to survive it and you're going to be okay, even in the worst-case scenario. You could lose money, financial stability or your reputation and still turn out okay. Even in the most unlikely situation, and even if all your worst fears materialize, you will be fine.

As you consider worst-case scenarios and what could possibly go wrong, consider what it would be like if you didn't do the thing you wanted to do. I didn't have to start a public blog or start coaching but I know that, at the end of my life, I would have regretted this badly. Imagine not pursuing your heart or your purpose. If you have had a strong message inside of you or a strong urge to sing a song or produce something, and you don't, you're not giving life to a dream living within you.

More painful than worst-case scenarios is regret. You get only one life to live. You can do this only once, so you might as well do the very thing you want to do. You don't want to be in your 80s and thinking that you should have gone for it. Imagine what that conversation with your younger self would look and feel like. Have that conversation with your younger self now and motivate your younger self to go for it. Remind the younger you that life is short and you don't want to sit in a bed of misery and regret later.

You don't know how things will work out. I get it. You could succeed, you think, or fail miserably. Well, if that's the case, why not take on the mindset of a scientist who is experimenting with life? Think of yourself as a cook in the kitchen who is merely trying out a new recipe to see if something will work. You're experimenting and trying out different hypotheses to test your theories about a project or business. If it works, you keep going. If it doesn't work, you try something different. If it doesn't work, you get someone else to help. If it doesn't work, you read up and experiment in a different way. Experiment your way through your fears. Failing or losing is simply a signal about how to do things better.

Another technique you can try – and one that my coach, Kristy, helped me use when I was battling my own fears of doing – is to note the different voices you hear within yourself. You're likely speaking to yourself throughout the day and you're hearing a couple of different voices from your consciousness. Some of the voices of fear you experience come from a lower-consciousness voice or from your worst fears. Within yourself, there are higher-consciousness voices that speak from a place of knowing, wisdom and purpose. When you doubt yourself and the lower-consciousness voices come out, write out – and remind yourself – of the higher-consciousness voices within you. Write down the wise and insightful things that you would be saying to yourself to overcome your doubts and fears.

Look behind the smallness of your fears and focus on the gravity of your purpose or mission. I could think to myself that it's embarrassing to put my divorce story out there when I write about my personal life. Who would ever tell people about how a marriage can be dysfunctional and how they had a big part to play in that relationship not working out? I really didn't want to say these things because it didn't make me look good to the outside world. Why air your dirty laundry in front of other people?

It was uncomfortable and unpleasant, yet I did it because my journey didn't stop there. I wanted to talk about marriage and the eventual divorce as a starting point. I wanted to show people there was a journey. You could go from your life's worst points to your life's highest. You could use rock bottom to bounce back. I had a deeper mission to convey to people and I was focused on living my life's purpose.

When you're thinking about the smallness of your fears, I challenge you to think about the larger purpose or mission of your life. When you hold onto the lofty and higher ideals of your life, the fears seem trivial. If you know what your life purpose is and if you're on this earth to achieve it, you'll do anything to overcome inner resistance. You will be able to set aside, overcome and transcend your fears. Focus on the bigness of your purpose and your life, not the smallness of the fears that are trying to trip you up.

All of these tips and strategies are for dealing with fear. My parting thought on fear is that you can have and feel fear while still going out and living your life. You can minimize fear, reduce its nose and lessen its impact on your life. There's nothing inherently wrong with fear; fear is part of being human. If you can recognize fear, acknowledge fear, set aside fear and do what you need to do, then you're still winning. You don't have to see the fear and allow it to stop you. You can acknowledge the fear and proceed.

14. Feeling Worth and Healing Wounds

Growing up in a negative and toxic environment at home impacted my self-worth. My father drove me to school every day and spent a lot of time complaining about his life and criticizing me. My mother wasn't a big fan of my achievements and regularly made sarcastic and hurtful comments.

If you're a plant (and you're not, since you're a human reading this book), growing up in toxic soil can be detrimental to your survival. It's like weeds or insects that eat away at your roots, bringing you to a quick death.

As humans, however, we must carry the heaviness throughout our lives. Self-worth can be deadly in not only keeping you stuck but lowering the overall quality of your life. You can achieve so much success if you simply believed in yourself and thought you could do it.

A statement that I will never forget is one from Warren Buffett. Someone once asked him about the most important thing in his life that had contributed to his success. If you can believe this, he said it was having an unconditionally loving upbringing and supportive parents. That alone can make someone into the world's wealthiest investor!

Feelings of unworthiness can make you feel like not starting, not doing, not finishing and not even trying. The worse your tank of self-worth, the more you'll find yourself stuck and procrastinating. You'll be afraid to launch your work and put yourself out there because of the perpetual fear of failure and what others will think of you. You'll play small, feel small and resist putting yourself out there.

I related all too well with this when it came to offering my coaching services and being on video. I just couldn't bring myself to do it, although I kept pushing myself to get out there. My entire set of videos on YouTube (more than 50 of them) is an experiment in courage and doing what I found uncomfortable. Every video was hard because I didn't want others to see me. However, I challenged myself to get up in front of the camera and speak my truth.

I don't know if I can dedicate only part of a chapter to self-worth and the work necessary to improve it. On Amazon, I have a couple of books about this topic, and they go into much more depth about how to love yourself, improve your self-worth and feel your worthiest self. Check out *The Self-Romance Manifesto* and *Love Yourself After Heartbreak* on Amazon.

If I was to share with you the essence of the practice, I would say it involves thinking about it in one of two ways. You must either re-parent yourself or treat yourself like a romantic partner. If you grew up in a difficult and challenging household, think about all the things your parents didn't do that you saw other parents do. Think about all the things your parents should have done or should have said to you. Speak to your inner child as if you were the mature adult parent. Give the lonely and hurting child within you the love and attention they need.

Re-parent the inner wounded child that is you. You must become your own parent and give your inner child the support and love they want.

Another way to think about increasing your self-worth is to treat yourself like your own romantic partner. You may have trouble loving yourself but you have no problem loving others. In fact, you may feel like you love others too much and give too much of yourself to the people you care about. To fill your own love tank, treat yourself as you would treat the person you care most about. Treat yourself like you would a romantic partner. Say the types of things, cultivate the kind of love and care for yourself the same way you would for someone who means a lot to you. Do the kinds of activities, care for yourself and support yourself exactly as you would for someone you are in love with.

Self-worth issues and other types of heavier wounding can feel heavy and slow down your ability to take action. The deeper emotional wounds of your life can be more weighty and paralyzing. If you suffered any kind of abuse, trauma, serious loss or episodes of pain, you're going to have a tough time getting out from under them. It may require therapy, counseling and much more help than I can offer in this book.

Deep emotional wounds get in your way and fill your mind, heart and soul with blocks, preventing you from moving forward. The work that you must do to clear the emotional blocks (I can offer you a roadmap more than step-by-step instructions here) is to fully get to the root of the problem. It's to acknowledge what you've experienced, face it and fully experience it without numbing it or reducing its significance to your life. It's to get the hurt out there and fully examine it. It's to feel the pain to its fullest intensity and cry it out completely.

Once the pain is out there and you have experienced it fully, it needs the compassionate ear of someone else. Someone else must hear and feel your pain. Having a sounding board or container that can share your pain with you is helpful in lowering the weight of the pain you're carrying around. Once you share with someone else, the next couple steps are to forgive the people who caused this pain you're experiencing. It's also to offer yourself forgiveness and compassion in healing.

Finally, to complete the healing, you need a story about your past hurt that is empowering and helpful to you. The idea is to see this event in your life in the most positive way possible, so you can move forward. It's to change the meaning of the event – from something that represents pain and suffering to something that represents growth, healing, learning and acceptance.

I know that a brief overview of emotional healing techniques isn't going to be enough to move on but it's a start. You may not be able to do this on your own, either. You may need the help of a professional or healer who can walk you through the process of letting go of the emotional pain burning in your heart. However, the one thing I can tell you is that despite the fact that the emotional pain is there, you can still go forward and use the techniques in this book.

Ideally, you are doing the deep inner work required to release the pain while taking necessary steps each day to move forward in your endeavors. Pain and moving forward can co-exist. You can be hurting and still do the things that you must do. The more you release the pain and the less heavy it becomes, the more you will coast in life. If you were cycling with a heavy backpack, it will now begin to feel like you're going downhill instead of uphill.

The better you get at managing the painful events in your life and increasing your self-worth, the freer you'll feel and the more energy you'll have to focus on the work in front of you. Don't let this pain, no matter how strong or severe it is, keep you from starting. If you have gone through something traumatic and painful, don't see your life as gloom and doom. Work on those inner core issues as you apply some of the more practical steps I'm outlining for you in these chapters.

15. Notice the Excuses

Your mind will get in the way and give you one excuse after another for why you can't do something.

In my own case, this happened for years until my divorce worked me up and made me realize that the only excuse for not starting my writing career was in my mind.

It might be helpful for you to list your excuses for not doing something. You will resist doing this because you won't actually believe that your excuses are excuses. When I work with some clients, they don't actually believe their excuses are excuses. They legitimately believe that something is a problem, obstacle, hindrance or impossibility.

I just don't believe that. I would go so far as to argue that any problem that comes between you and the thing you want has only two resolutions: an excuse or a solution.

Any problem, any obstacle or any challenge that you don't address or that you don't have a solution for is an excuse.

At the end of the day, you have to take responsibility for achieving what you want to achieve. If you take the power away from the circumstances of life or the universe, you realize that you are more directly involved in the outcome. You have the power to make things happen – or to make them not happen. Something is an excuse or obstacle only if you say it is. If you fully embrace your power and responsibility in whatever you face, you won't let excuses run the day. If you take ultimate responsibility for everything, you won't feel like you're unable to change the direction in which things are moving.

It's impossible only if your mind makes it so. My clients tend to believe that something is too expensive, too uncertain, too soon, too late, too far away or too big of a risk. As they explain to me the issue they're facing and why it's hard for them to achieve what they want to achieve, I just hear various degrees of excuses.

Let's say you legitimately have an excuse for why you can't do something. Write it down and then offer 10 different solutions on paper. Brainstorm a few realistic ideas and a few impractical ideas to help you see that solutions are out there. When your brain gets into solution-finding mode, it will be less stuck on the excuses.

Once you have a list of ways to solve the problem, focus on the action items or to-do items. It's not that something is impossible; you just may have to work towards solving it. Let's say you don't have any time to work on your passion project or side hustle due to the commitments of your job or family. Your excuse can be that you don't have time. Yet, you likely do have time that you're not paying attention to. There are a couple hours of internet or social media time that you can cut out of your life. There is likely time during your lunch hour and later at night when the kids are asleep. You may not have time at first glance, but you'll have to take action to create time.

If you focus on the action items for creating more time, you may need a schedule. You may need to do a little better job planning. You may need to bring in other people – relatives or neighbors – to give yourself some time to create space in your schedule. The idea isn't to stay focused on the problem or the excuse so you can look for ways to avoid doing something. Instead, it's to actively look for ways to overcome the excuse at hand.

Rebut those excuses. For any problem, look at the solution and the possible ways to get around the problem. Set up an action plan containing things you can do to get around that problem. Work on the solutions instead of fixating on the problem.

Look past the problems and excuses and towards the prize. Look at the final outcome, goal or target. Sometimes, focusing on the immediate will make completion seem challenging. The problems and excuses will pop out at you but if you can look a little beyond today and at least see what's possible, you will reduce the problems as well as your excuses for not addressing them.

If you can focus on a clearer picture of the future, the excuses will seem minuscule. The bigger the vision, the smaller the accompanying excuses. Focusing on what you want and what it will feel like to get it will help you put excuses in their place. The excuses will seem irrelevant and tiny compared to the thing you're pursuing. Excuses get in the way and block your path. You can overcome them by sticking to your vision.

Your attitude is key. Some people see obstacles and challenges as hindrances that prevent them from getting to where they want to go. You can choose to see them as hurdles or, even better, as launching pads. Use excuses to address problems, get a better understanding and launch yourself on to the next step. Challenges arise to guide you, test you and help you perfect your journey. If you view obstacles this way, they can only help you proceed. Seeing obstacles as dead ends and uphill battles will result in a much more treacherous road ahead.

Remember, the choice of attitude is in your hands and you can change it today. You can look for the problems or you can see the problems as opportunities rather than as excuses.

When confronting challenges, instead of asking, "Why is the universe punishing me?" or "Why is this so difficult?," ask yourself, "How is this here for my learning and growth? How is this helping me get to where I need to go?"

16. Bounce Back From Your Failures

I went through a devastating divorce and breakup. It was life-altering and made me question the meaning of life itself. It took me years to get out of it. I won't bore you with the details here but if you need an additional million words of reading, check out my blog on this topic, where I chronicled my pain in more detail. You can see more at www.vishnusvirtues.com. I also published several – yes, several – books on the topic of divorce and moving on.

I bring this up here because it was one of the greatest personal failures and disappointments in my life. Everyone I know came to know of this divorce. They came to know that my relationship had ended, that I had experienced rejection in some way and that I had struggled with interpersonal relationships. When one goes through something like a divorce or breakup, people come to think that something is wrong with that person. It was a personal and public failure.

Yet, after the divorce, I had to find a way to move on and meet people again, to move forward. Taking action after a major failure like this was impossible. I had failed in an important area of my life and now I would have to go forward and redo it. I would have to start meeting people again, go out and dates, try out new relationships and put myself out there. I, of course, felt paralyzed and stuck in the past for years. I could move forward a few steps at a time but then I took many steps back.

I want to share with you how to go forward after experiencing a major failure in your own life. You start by learning about the past failure so you won't repeat the mistakes. If you can switch your focus from pain to learning, you won't focus on the pain of failing; rather, you will focus on learning and figuring out what went wrong. Think about the things that didn't work, that you royally screwed up on and that you shouldn't do again in the future.

I had no idea about marriage. I had no idea about relationships. I had no idea about being vulnerable. I had no idea about being emotionally open. I have to admit that I royally screwed up in my marriage and I feel bad for my ex for having to endure this relationship with someone who was clueless and stubborn about making any kind of change. Yet, now I can reflect on this experience and enroll in the university of learning. I know how to not be a terrible partner in a relationship! I know what it takes to make relationships work. I know all the things not to do. If you can look at your past failure and get to the lessons, you're moving in the right direction.

You can choose to see the past experience as something that was negative or devastating or you can try hard to see how the experience positively affected your life. I could have gotten hung up on what a complete devastation my life was because of my marriage. Honestly, I did think this way for a few years of my life, which kept me from doing too much. However, once I started seeing this, I started asking life's big questions, understanding myself better, discovering who I was spiritually and learning how to be better at relationships, I knew that this portion of my life was the game-changer. It even inspired me to pursue my calling and start doing work I would have never imagined doing before.

What was your biggest failure? What did you learn from it? How did that failure improve your life? Yes, you can give me lots of answers about how it destroyed your life but how did it improve your life? How did you become a better person because of it? Reflect on every positive thing that came out of the failure. Once you create a list of positives versus negatives, notice how many more good things your failure led you to. Keep your focus on the positive aspects of that failed experience so you will feel inspired to move forward on the project at hand.

Failure gives you a unique outlook on how to not do something, so don't lose your perspective on that. Like I said, being a failure in marriage wasn't all for nothing because I learned about the many things I did wrong. If you start a business that failed terribly, your next business will not start at ground zero because you will know what didn't work. You will avoid all your past mistakes, make better decisions and be sitting on a wealth of experience. Your failures show you what to avoid and what not to do, so don't ignore the power of failure in your life. You have an insider's advantage because you know what didn't work. Other business owners who failed may not even give the venture another try or may not take their experiences into account for the next venture. However, if you are mindful and aware of this, you will do so.

Once you get past that failure, I hope you realize that you can get through any failure. In a way, you can already get past all failures you have encountered in your life. Think about it. You were able to turn every lemon in your life into the sweet-tasting lemonade you're enjoying today. You have resiliency, which is another superpower. The mantras here are, "I can succeed well because I have failed well," and "I can get through any failure because I have done it over and over and over again." You have. Each time something fell apart, you have picked yourself up, re-invented, re-created and come out swinging once again. Know the power of your resiliency and remind yourself that you have the ability to encounter any failure and overcome it.

Thus, if you are stuck in the failures of your past or fearing your failures in the future, which is slowing you down, know that you will win either way. You have gotten over the past failures and if you fail again, you will bounce back. Also, as far as the future is concerned, if you fail, you will learn to bounce back from that failure because you have experience doing it. You are not a quitter. You keep going even in the face of failure and disappointment. Failure isn't your setback; you know that overcoming failure is your secret weapon for success.

Another way to see failure is as a test. Because I failed profoundly at marriage and relationships, I now had a test in front of me, to determine whether I still wanted this despite everything that had happened. Yes, I did. You can see if failing at your project or business is a game-ending failure or a game-changing one. Is it over or are you still motivated and inspired to move forward? Use failure to determine whether it's something you really want out of life. Use failure as a test to check your resolve. If it's not worth it, you'll give up on it. If it is worth it, you'll keep writing books. Speaking about myself here (and my authorship journey. I could have given up after some mediocre successes on books but I loved it and chose to keep going. I'm hoping that the quality of my books and of my reflections on life keep improving, too.

If you experienced a major failure and are starting over, here are some thoughts. Do it differently this time. Have a plan to avoid making the same mistakes. Approach the situation with more strategy than you did before. If you failed, you know what to look out for and you can be more intentional in the work you're doing this time. You can decide ahead of time what resources you need and how to get them. You can decide ahead of time on the marketing and sales strategies. You can decide ahead of time how to spend money, where to pick up equipment and where to set up shop.

Also, think about a team supporting you – the people whom you need to do the work that you need to do. If you're an author, you need an editor, a publisher and someone who does your marketing. You could do all that but it's better to do the things you're better at doing and allowing others to handle the rest. If you're starting a business, you need to do the part you're good at and find a team to support you. You may need legal, accounting, branding and marketing help. You don't have to go it alone. Think about a team so the journey is less lonely and you feel more supported.

Why is it that the most famous people in the world are all experts at failure? They have used every idea I've mentioned here to come out stronger in the end. When something they did failed, like Apple products or the first airplane, they didn't give up. They kept trying to figure out what went wrong, what didn't work and what could work better. They learned and tried again. They thought ahead, planned and got a support team. They looked at the positives that came out of the failure and went with it.

Most importantly, and I'm going to leave this with you in closing, they didn't give up. They realized that if they stayed the course and kept moving forward, victory was theirs. I know it will be the same for you, too. Perseverance is underrated but the people who stay with something, who keep getting better at it and who keep failing, no matter how bad things get, are the ones who succeed. Every famous politician failed and lost elections before becoming the leader of their respective countries. Many athletes fail in their careers before becoming world-famous. The examples – from people to products to fast food chains – are all around you. The key to success is failing often, failing well and failing with learning. Use failure to your advantage. Fail forward, not backward, and keep going.

17. Find Your Inner Motivation

It's easy to get motivation from the outside. If someone promises to give you fame, money, a car or some other monetary reward, you'll do what they want. We pursue education to get good grades to get a good job to get a good salary.

You do something to get something in return. Most of the time, this is something on the outside. It's an exchange of your time, energy or abilities to receive praise, notoriety or compensation. There's nothing wrong with this except you may lose interest in the external rewards and, therefore, lose your desire to do things altogether.

I'm a proponent of doing things for the enjoyment of doing them. This is what will help you jump out of bed in the morning to do the things you want to do. I remember two different situations in my life that had to do with sleeping. When I was practicing criminal defense law, I tried to sleep a lot and stay in bed. I was very resistant to doing this work of helping defend people who had been accused of crimes. It didn't align with my value system and I wasn't into it. Why did I show up for work? Because it was a job and I was getting money to do it. It paid for my rent and it supported my ex-wife and me. Simple.

I eventually quit that job and later started an online immigration law firm. When I opened this firm, I found my clients to be fiancés and spouses who had gotten married and then immigrated to the United States. As readers of my relationship blog might know, I have a passion for this subject. Having gone through heartache and heartbreak, I enjoyed bringing couples together and helping them unite as a family. It brought me profound satisfaction to know I could help my clients navigate the immigration system and be together. I felt partially responsible for, or part of, their love story.

The difference was like night and day. I was out of bed in a minute each morning to go to work on my cases and help my clients. I took phone calls anytime and responded to emails quickly. I listened to clients' problems with empathy and a keen eye towards helping them resolve their situations. I couldn't wait to do the work because I truly enjoyed it. It wasn't even because of the legal aspects of this job but because I could unite loved ones and couples. What a satisfying job!

Also, what an internally motivating job. I enjoyed it simply because I enjoyed it. So much of our lives, we find ourselves "forced" to do things we really don't care about. Even if you like your job, you have to motivate yourself to do it because it's not the most fulfilling thing in the world. We also live here in the practical world, so we can't completely afford to just do what we want and avoid everything else.

Except, my two cents to you is that we can. Not 100% and not every day but there is a way. If you decide that you're going to do only work that is internally satisfying and motivating, you can set the intention to do that today. I'm not 100% there yet but I'm no longer doing work in the legal field that was very externally motivating. Instead, I moving towards doing creative work and work that helps people through my writing, which is extremely internally motivating.

As of the time of this writing, I work in the world of NGOs in the United States. Soon, however, I will be leaving this job to work on my writing and coaching full time. This work is super internally motivating. I stay up late to do this work. I wake up early to do this work. I find every free minute I can to write content, create blog posts, make videos on Instagram and support people any way I can. I cannot imagine doing this work full time but I can. Having worked on these projects for years, I feel more and more like I can do this as my primary work. Never would I have imagined that I could have the life I wanted by doing the thing I wanted to do. You, too, can get to where you want to be by going with the thing that motivates you internally.

I am encouraging you to do work that is more internally fulfilling and satisfying. The way to do more internally aligned work is to know yourself better and to read Part 3 of this book, which contains ideas on how to live in alignment with your passions, purpose and principles. When you do work that you intrinsically enjoy, you won't have to work another day in your life. You won't have to struggle with paralysis or procrastination if you can jump out of bed and do the work you're meant to be doing.

What is that one job or occupation you can see yourself doing and you don't need to even read this book to do it? You wouldn't be stuck, you wouldn't feel resistance and you wouldn't have any trouble doing it with excitement and joy? Whatever your answer is, it's what you should be moving towards. Yes, you're going to have plenty of objections and calls to return to reality but reality is what you make of it. If you can't do something now, start planning. If you can't go all in, do it as a side hustle. If you can't do it as a side hustle, do it for 15 minutes a day. Just start with the intention of doing it.

To figure out what other things motivate you internally, reflect on these concepts. What is it that you enjoy doing for the pure joy of it, without any need for external rewards? What makes you happy and joyful? Yes, this can be art, hobbies and sports as well. Whatever you come up with doesn't have to make money or support you. I would simply encourage you to figure this out because I believe that the more you engage in internally satisfying activities, the more this satisfaction will flow over into the work you do with external rewards.

In addition to what sets you on fire, what is it you're lukewarm about and would rather stay in bed and not do? Knowing what to stay away from or what doesn't light your fire is great insider information. The more you know what doesn't satisfy you and what doesn't light your fire, the closer you get to the things that do. Also, if you believe that knowing this information is only going to frustrate you because it's your day job, don't fear. There's a way out, no matter what you think or believe. If you need some support or coaching, reach out and get in touch.

In addition to knowing what sets you on fire and what doesn't, reflect on what would happen if you didn't do the thing you were supposed to be doing. How much regret would you have later if you didn't pursue the life you could have pursued? What would not following your entrepreneurial dream or creative endeavors mean to you if you never got started on them? Consider what regret would do to you as a way to get clearer on what to do with your life.

You can do things that are internally motivating if they bring you joy and pleasure. This doesn't take much work and you know what these things are without having to think too much. Another way to find internal motivation is through mastery. People are motivated to do things so that they can get better at them. Whether it's singing or coding, people find pleasure in improving at their craft or work.

You can become internally motivated out of curiosity and interest. You may feel like you want to learn everything about a subject and become an expert on it, which will help you stay internally motivated. Or challenging situations and circumstances can help you stay internally motivated. Dealing with problems, overcoming problems and fixing problems in your projects may be what motivates you. Finding challenges and obstacles in the work they do motivates some people to keep going at it. Some people run away from workplace challenges while others run towards them.

A final reminder that a lot of internal motivation can come from giving and service. Giving to other people makes you feel like you're on top of the world. It's why people who are in the service professions – and I'm including myself here as a writer – feel supremely motivated. It's why nurses, teachers and firefighters love their jobs. It's not so much that they like doing all aspects of their jobs but that they are passionate about helping other people. That's because helping others feels good even if you're not getting a paycheck for it. Use service and giving as ways to motivate yourself to do more with less resistance.

Fame, power, money and notoriety work for politicians and mob bosses but likely not for you. You're not going to stay motivated and focused if you follow those external things. Even if you are, you won't feel fulfilled or as though what you're doing matters. It will cause you to pause and experience many of the struggles with resistance that I've written about in this book.

For more internal motivation ideas, get ready for Part 3. Each chapter explores ways to be productive and active by connecting with more important underlying principles. Once you can tie your work to your values, life principles, passion, purpose and emotions, the work in front of you will not feel like work. There is nothing wrong with moving away from work that you're not passionate about and moving towards work that is more personally satisfying. If personally satisfying work will help you be more productive and successful in the long run, it's what you should be striving towards.

Part 3.

Go After the Life You Want

18. Connect With Your Life's Purpose

Staying focused on your life's purpose will help you keep moving forward. It will help you break the resistance when you feel paralyzed.

Do you just wake up one day and find yourself awakened to your purpose? Not quite (though some people do). People who have experienced a profound event or a significant circumstance in their lives tend to figure out their purpose pretty quickly. Others may be floating through life not knowing what their purpose is.

For me, one of the easiest ways to discover my life purpose was through a painful experience. The stuff they say about finding purpose in your pain is not a cliché! I've known many people who have found their life's work through the struggles and painful experiences they've gone through. People who have had relatives in the medical system that failed them have become medical professionals. People who have lost someone to disease or tragedy have become advocates for those very causes. People who have experienced certain kinds of setbacks as children (being a foster kid, moving a lot, struggling in academics) have found a way to make it their life's mission to improve those conditions.

Think about the greatest pain you've ever experienced. It's not a bad thing if you've experienced a relatively pain-free life. What other struggles have you experienced? If you can go through your life and think about the struggles or pain you've experienced, this is a starting point. Next, think about the lessons and wisdom you gained out of that experience. What message did that experience send to you? What are you supposed to do with your life based on that experience? Go through each experience you've had and reflect on which one speaks to you to the loudest. Which one has seeds of your purpose in it? Which ones don't?

One key to figuring out your life's purpose is eliminating all those things that are not your life's purpose. This is one of my favorite life strategies. You may not know what your purpose is or what you're supposed to be doing with your life but you can deduce this by figuring out what you don't want to do. If your purpose isn't to be an entrepreneur, writer, creative, influencer, activist or artist, what is it? When you take many options and many life purposes off the table, you're left with only a couple options. Knowing what you don't want in your life and knowing what your life purpose isn't is one way to figure out what your life purpose is or could be. Use the method of getting rid of things that are not your life purpose to help you figure out what your purpose is.

I would argue that all of us, at some level, know what our purpose is. I don't think the problem is knowing; rather, it's awareness. Most of your life, you've been going about doing certain things and you don't even realize what you're doing.

I'll try to show you what I mean. When I was in high school and college, I was involved in social service clubs, which meant doing volunteer work for other people. When I graduated, for some reason, I never got jobs in the corporate world. Following is a list of the jobs I had. I worked for workers, helping them organize to form unions or representing them if they had a union. I worked as a lawyer, representing workers, helping injured people and helping people go through divorces. I started a business that helped immigrants get visas and green cards to the US. I worked for a non-profit, helping advocate for seniors and the elderly. I also started coaching divorcees and people who had gone through a breakup.

If you take each of those jobs on its own, you won't be able to see the connection and how it's related to purpose. Yet, now that you have learned about all these jobs, you know that my purpose is to help people in difficult situations. It's what I've always been drawn to. Not just your typical "I'm having a bad day," but people who are in seriously difficult situations. People who are forced to flee their countries as immigrants, people who are facing the possibility of spending a lot of time in jail, people who are facing punishment or losing their jobs for trying to organize in the workplace. Each type of job helped people in the direst of situations.

I believe that my life's purpose is to help people in dire situations transform their lives and use their adversity to their advantage. I came to this conclusion after interpreting my life and my life events. Nothing brings me as much joy as leading people on this journey from adversity to achievement and excellence. When others run away from the hard stuff, I run towards it, knowing that opportunity and possibility are there. All great things start when things fall apart.

Your life journey has a purpose. One of the interesting things you get to do is review your life, look for the different clues in each step of the journey and put together the pieces. It's not that you don't have a life purpose. You have a life purpose. It isn't that you have to pull your life purpose out of thin air. You just have to discover what is already there.

You have to put the pieces together like a puzzle, to analyze and interpret what your life is telling you. The good news is that it has been telling you your life purpose for a long time. Life is screaming your life purpose to you. All you have to do is listen to what it's saying.

Understand your purpose by looking at it as a journey. This activity will help. Note every job you've had in your life. Include jobs you received payment for, work you did for other people in your life and community work you did as a volunteer. Reflect on each job. If you can write down your purpose for doing that job, do so. Now that you have a list of the work you've done, as well as the activities you've done outside work, along with their purposes written next to them, go through the various life purpose statements you've written and analyze them. Look at what they all have in common; find similar themes and a central concept. Just like figuring out a puzzle, your life purpose will pop out at you.

Knowing your life purpose will serve as a reminder when you're working on projects. Ideally, your projects are in alignment with your purpose. If they are not, you may want to reflect on whether they're worth doing. If a project is not in alignment, can you bring it in alignment with your purpose? Can you focus on parts of your project that are more in alignment with who you are and hand off the other tasks to someone else?

The more in alignment you are with your purpose, the less likely you are to face resistance and struggle.

19. What Is Your Life's Message?

Along the same lines of life purpose, your life's message, or life's meaning, are powerful forces that can help you break free of the resistance you're facing.

These are ideas I've picked up from my work as a coach to help people determine what their life's work and message is.

A couple concepts to think through. If you were going to write on that famous billboard and send a message to the world, what would you write to the world about life or work or business? What would you say to the world in a professional context? What would you say to the world in your personal life?

If I were doing this exercise, I would say to the world, "Your setbacks are a setup to your best life" or "Let your adversity be the launching pad to your success." For me, in my professional and personal lives, I gravitated towards people in dire circumstances and helped them find relief from them or to improve on them.

In my recent work doing relationship coaching, I tell my clients, "Your breakup can be the catalyst to your best life and your best relationship." It's similar to the ideas I've been sharing here in this book. For example, in the last chapter on purpose, I said that knowing what your life purpose isn't can help you determine what your life purpose is.

Similarly, my message is that getting things profoundly wrong and not knowing what works is the step to understanding and knowing what does. You can't know the light if you don't know the darkness.

What is your message? What would message you would write on a billboard on the freeway, for the world to see? What would be the 10-15 word reminder you would like the world to know? If thinking about a billboard doesn't inspire you, what would you write on your tombstone or what would you write as your final message to the world? It's your final days of life and you have to leave behind something profound and wise. For you, what would that be?

Or if you're the creative type, let's say you are going to receive the top award in your platform. You are going on stage to collect the Emmy, the Grammy, the Oscar or some other high honor. You are going to have the opportunity to share some words with the audience and your speech must be impactful. If you are not in the creative arena, imagine you are attending a graduation at Harvard University. Yes, you're Oprah and you've received an invitation to Harvard. You have a moment in time to leave your legacy for the world. Your words will be taped, televised and recorded for history. They will be your lasting legacy for the world and will be what people remember about you.

Have I built up enough anticipation or invited you to elevate the importance of this speech? Good. Write out this speech now. Write your message, meaning, purpose, wisdom and guidance for your audience and the world. Within your speech and what you're about to come up with are the deepest truths you hold and the wisest knowledge you have. This is your legacy and what you stand for.

This may be harder than you imagine. You may have written out your message but you have no idea if this message resonates with you. You know how a message resonates? It's so powerful that it makes you get out of bed in the morning and jump to your work. You're excited to wake up, get up and get to work because you have a message to deliver to the world. The message is so powerful that it helps you transcend any limitation to get up and do it.

I was recently working with someone who had a hard time figuring out his message. I had him write down his message every morning for a week. He wrote one message for his business and one message for his life. He didn't have to look at the previous day's message; he just had to write the message he felt each day. At the end of the week, I had him go through the messages and pull out the one that resonated the most with him.

How do you know when you've landed on a powerful message? It will make you jump out of bed in the morning and work on it. For example, the client is a runner, so he gets excited about jumping out of bed and going for a run. I asked him to find a message that resonated with him so deeply that he wanted to get out of bed in the morning so that he could create content and services for the people he serves. It can be as simple as the fact that you want people to live a healthy life or be more fulfilled. Remember, if it's not causing you to jump out of bed or stay awake late into the night to work on it, it's not the best message for you. The best message for you is a message that you feel drawn to, that resonates with you and inspires you to sleep less, jump out of bed in the morning and spread your message more.

Another technique that I mentioned in the previous section on finding your life purpose is to go through your life events and circumstances.

Previously, I had you look at every job you held and discover what that job's message was. Now go through your positive and negative life experiences and discover the message behind each of them. If you started a business, what was the message? If you closed a business, what was the message? If you traveled around the world, what was the message? If you did some volunteer work that significantly changed your life, what was the message? If you had a painful breakup or divorce, what was the message?

Collect the various life messages from the different circumstances of your life and write them down. Once again, you'll begin to see similarities and themes. Life has been continuously communicating with you but you haven't figured out how to listen to it. This is how. You acknowledge the events in your life. You listen to the messages that life has sent out. You acknowledge the messages. Then, you find the common themes among these messages and, finally, come up with the strongest message – the one that resonates most with you. Once you have figured out this message, see how you think about it and feel about it. Does it move you? Does it excite you? Do you want to share it with the world? First message, then action. Often, people take action without knowing why they're doing it. If you know your why, you can accomplish just about anything in the world.

Now, that you have figured this out ahead of time, start living this message today. You know your life philosophy and message, so your job in life is to live in alignment with it. Put this up on the wall and remind yourself that this is who you are and what you stand for. Then, every day, take inspired action based on this life principle and life message. Do things based on this underlying life message. Write, create, speak and pursue opportunities that align with this life message. The more on-message you live your life, the more productive and fulfilled you'll be.

20. Become Your Own Coach

In this book, I've talked about many exercises that will help you get clearer on your vision, your purpose and your meaning in life. I want you to know that if you get clear on your mission and purpose, there's no slowing you down. Yet, while you may know your mission and purpose, you might still feel stuck. You may know why you're here on earth and still be struggling to do the work that you were put here to do. What's the deal?

Simply, you forget. Ha. Yes, the explanation can be as easy as that. See, we humans are always on the hunt for knowledge, information and insight. You are always looking for the truth, looking for answers and looking for the meaning of life. You're searching so much that when you find the truth, you forget and move on.

You need a reminder and you need conditioning so you don't forget the lessons you've learned. This requires repetition and practice, just like an athlete on the field. Someone who is after the gold medal in the Olympics doesn't prepare just occasionally. They prepare for years of their life and they know exactly which medal they are going after.

They wake up in the morning and focus on the medal until they go to sleep at night. They focus on their dreams. They focus on their life's mission. It's not about the gold medal, either. It's about becoming the best version of themselves. It's about breaking through their own mental blocks and inner barriers to achieve their potential in life.

Top world athletes and performers likely have doubts and insecurities as well. They may find it hard to get out of bed every morning and perform but they are constantly reminding themselves about what's at stake and why they are doing what it is they want.

I want you to get into the daily habit of reminding yourself about what it is you want. I want you to keep in mind your purpose, your reasons, your dream and your outcome. I want you to get clear on why you're doing whatever it is you're doing. Yes, you need to become your own coach.

What is your purpose? What is your meaning? What are your principles or values, as you're going to read about next. What is your why? What is the most powerful reason why you're doing what you're doing?

Asking myself these questions, I realized that I am doing what I'm doing to help people, to assist them in moving away from the place where they are stuck, in life or in relationships, and to a much better place in their lives. I am using my voice, my writing, my appearance on videos and podcasts to help people break free from the places where they are stuck. People leaving one place for another and transforming their lives is what brings me joy.

Also, on a personal level, the ability to work on my own terms, doing work that I am passionate about and from anywhere in the world also brings me joy. I don't have to follow the rules of an employer or a company. I don't have a boss or a manager. I work best unsupervised and with complete access to my own time. This absolute freedom of time is what excites me and keeps me going.

The underlying joy in my life is the ability to work on my own schedule and to create and produce content, books and other helpful materials. The reason I do these things is to help people overcome adversity and transform their lives. I value growth and spirituality. To me, growth is spirituality. People growing is a spiritual practice.

This is why I do what I do and it's what I'm most passionate about. Each day, I remind myself that this is what it's all about for me. This is how I'm able to get up day after day and focus on my mission of helping and serving others. I make the case to myself that my words can heal, help and transform others. I recognize that this work is creating growth for both myself and others. It's a spiritual practice. I remind myself that doing this work will give me the freedom of time and location that allows me to work best.

These are my reasons, and as my own coach, I make this case to myself. I repeat these reasons to myself every day and make this case when I am facing procrastination or resistance. I tell myself that this is what I want and what I would get out of it by doing the work.

Of course, my mind easily forgets what I want. "Shiny object syndrome" causes it to become bored and distracted. It's like a puppy that runs towards something new every day. It makes me look up things, like how to become a fiction author or how to leave my present-day life and become a monk. My job, then, is to go back and remind myself about what it is I want and why it is I want it.

Once you know what you want and why you want it, ritualize it. Symbolize it by turning some object or item you own into a representation of your life's dreams and desires. Write it down and affirm it to yourself on the daily. Then, like a coach, cheerleader or your own lawyer, remind yourself about the reasons why you're doing what you're doing.

Remind yourself that this is furthering your greatest life purpose. It's aligning with your values and principles. It'll create the life you want. Your work today will design your vision tomorrow. You don't have time to sleep or slack. It's time to get up and get going.

When the negative thoughts of sabotage or disinterest show up, you'll have to step in as your own coach. You'll have to tell the self-sabotaging thoughts that they hold no power over you. You'll have to bring up your most intense desires and dreams and show the negative thoughts that you will prevail. An inner battle is going on. The coach of your dreams and purpose needs to win for the sake of your life.

Activate your coach's heart. Cultivate this coach for your dreams. Keep reminding yourself what it is you want and why it is you're doing what you're doing. Out-coach and out-motivate the voices of negativity and distraction that are trying to lead you astray.

Stay focused on the destination and keep going. Your future is awaiting your arrival.

21. Craft Your Ideal Day Today

What would it be like to live your ideal day? You don't have to put this off into the future. You can start on this today to get some clarity on what your ideal day would look like. To be clear, it's not what it should look like or how you can reorganize your typical day to fit what works for you.

This idea is important because it's hard to live a life that's true to you when someone else's schedule is controlling you. Think about this. You dedicate 8 hours of your day to sleep. Ten hours is for work and in your workplace. You have control over only the other 6 hours of your life. Can you believe that? You can control only 6 hours of your life.

Within those 6 hours, you have little time to get motivated, inspired and live the life you want to live. You are living your life around your work and sleep schedule, not creating your work and sleep schedule around your life.

Before you start saying that this is crazy talk and I'm living in a dream, bear with me. I don't want you to think about all the reasons why this is a preposterous idea or why you can't create your ideal day and life. I don't want you to shut down this idea because it's too unrealistic. I don't want you to shut down this idea because you've been in some job for 20 years and plan to be there for another 10 years.

I want you to go beyond your current circumstances. Forget about your current everyday reality. Forget about what you do on a daily basis. Forget about work schedules, children's schedules and any other time limitations you have. I want you to detach yourself from reality at the moment and go into a space where you can envision and dream. I want you to be able to visualize and see your life without looking around at the reality of today.

I did this shortly after my divorce. I imagined what my ideal life would be like. I didn't take work or reality or practicality into account. I want you to notice how improbable this can be in the real world and then notice that I was somewhat able to achieve it, even if my ideal life seemed highly unrealistic and improbable.

I imagined a day when I would wake up, work on my craft and engage in writing and creating. No schedule would govern me and I would be able to prioritize creativity, spirituality and peace. My paid work would be secondary and would work around my creative work. This is the life I had imagined.

Soon after that, I got a job with an NGO that allowed me to work from home, create my own schedule and prioritize my day. It was a 40-hour-a-week job but I could spread that out based on my own schedule. I could work evenings and weekends if I wanted. I could start my day at 9 am or 12 noon as long as I was doing the 40 hours. It was also a job advocating for senior citizens, which I absolutely loved.

The even-better part was that I could wake up early and start on my writing projects at 5 in the morning, get ready and then leisurely start my "day job." I could do coaching throughout the day when I had clients and then return to my more flexible NGO work when I had the time. On top of scheduling creativity and having a more stable income, I could exercise at my convenience, go to the gym at my convenience and meditate at my convenience.

I woke up every day thinking to myself that I was living a dream. I had complete time freedom, which made me feel like a millionaire. On top of it all, the job allowed me to take several months off at a time. I traveled overseas and, once again, was able to design my life exactly as I wanted it. I could create my own schedule and fill my day with creativity, spirituality and service.

Now that I am moving on to write and coach full time and leaving the NGO work behind, I have my own schedule back to create the life I want. I just did not imagine that it was possible to have a job for which you didn't have to go to an office every day. I didn't think you could have a job in which your boss wasn't in the same office as you were and asking you for a strict accountability of your time.

What do you want your ideal day to look like? What would you do during the day? How would you feel during the day? Nothing that you have in your life now has to be there, except, of course, your spouse, the little people in your life and anyone you live with. Even if there are people around you and who depend on you, you can still create an ideal day. Break away from the reality of today's circumstances and daydream a little bit. Think about what your perfect day would look and feel like.

Now that you have this in mind, I have a challenge for you. Can you create that one ideal day today, just to get a taste of it? You may not be able to do that idea day tomorrow but can you take some time to plan it? Even if it's a week or two down the road and even if it's for only one day? If you can't just plan one ideal day, how can you live one ideal day?

We have grown up believing that certain things, like schedules and work, are out of our hands. I'm challenging you to rethink that. Never in a million years did I think I could work from where I wanted to work, and on my own schedule, but my NGO job offered just that opportunity. If that wasn't enough, after I left this job, I was able to completely design my schedule and my time.

Don't wait until you get there to create the life you want. Create the life you want today. You may not be able to live that life completely right now but you can start. You can design your day off, your weekend and be able to plan where you will work from.

22. Live in Alignment With Your Principles

There was a time in my life when I could hardly get out of bed and go to work. I had to walk into courtrooms, lawyers' offices and law libraries but it was so difficult. I could have tried many of the ideas I've outlined in this book (and trust me, I did) but an overwhelming resistance kept me from doing what I had to do.

This book is about doing the work you want to do and feel called to do but are struggling to do because of internal resistance. But what if you weren't meant to do it, you weren't called to do it and it isn't what you want to do? In one very simple word, don't.

You don't have to do things you absolutely don't want to do. If you're protesting because you feel there are many things you have to try doing out of obligation, this chapter is especially for you. The idea is to break free, reduce your commitments and get out of things that are not meant for you.

If you think this is impossible, I would say that your thinking is what makes it impossible. If you think you are obligated to your family, kids, house and mortgage, I would suggest taking a step back and seeing what in this process you do have control over. What can you change? What can you stop doing? What can you move around?

You don't have to accept the default life. Yes, change is uncomfortable at times but you have options. If you don't like your job, you can transition out of your high-paying job to a more balanced, lower-paying one. If you feel like you're in debt and overwhelmed financially, you can cut down on your monthly expenses and change what you're spending money on. If you live in an expensive part of town, you can move. If you don't like the fact that you have a long commute, you can change where or how you work.

Let's say you don't know what you want and what you're supposed to be doing in the first place. In that case, it's time to look at your life principles. These are the foundational principles that govern your life but that you're probably not paying attention to. Some people call them "values." These principles (or values) are the very things that run your life but you don't recognize them or even know they exist.

What are the different principles that govern our lives? Perhaps creativity, spirituality or kindness govern you. Imagine if these were some of your life principles and you were a lawyer. Exactly! That's why I found it challenging to be a lawyer. There's not much room for creativity or spirituality when one is practicing law. There's not much room for kindness or compassion when one is dealing with difficult lawyers or imposing judges.

If you're living a life that's contrary to your principles, a lot of what you're doing will be an uphill battle. I encourage you to examine whether you're stuck because of inner resistance or because you're doing things you're not supposed be doing with your life. Are you not living in alignment with your life principles and values?

To make this determination, consider what is important to you. Step back and think about the principles that are important to you in your life. Check online for a list of different principles governing life. Common values include authenticity, fairness, family, freedom, creativity, spirituality, fun, gratitude, justice, humor, patience, trust, passion, etc.

Each of these life principles is governing your life. Find the 3-5 principles that most resonate with you. When I work with clients, getting clear on this is one of the most important things I help them understand. Once they – and you – realize what values are governing their (your) life, future decisions become easy. Well, it gets hard at first because you may realize that you're living your life in contrast to the principles governing your life.

Your life is meaningful and fulfilling when you're living in alignment with your principles. You are also productive and effective when you're living in alignment with the principles you value. Life's too short to do things for the sake of doing them or to force yourself to accomplish tasks that are not in alignment with what's important to you.

Maybe you're so used to living a default life, you haven't had a chance to step back and ask yourself the deeper questions. Is this what I really want? Is this what's important to me? Do I have a choice about what I'm doing? Do I not have to do this? Can I make changes?

If you're in alignment with the life you want and doing the things you're supposed to be doing and you're still facing resistance, use the strategies in this book. If you're struggling with something because it's not in alignment with the life you want or it's not what you want to do, step back and get more curious about the bigger resistance. You can resist procrastination and fear but you shouldn't resist your life path or your underlying life principles.

If you're going against your principles, you don't know yourself well enough. You need much deeper introspection, reflection and awareness. If you're not living your life principles because you didn't know that certain principles were governing your life, take some time to see if this is the life you want, if this is the project you want or if this is the path you want to take.

In my book *7 Sacred Promises*, I wrote about these much bigger issues in life. They will help you live with more meaning and purpose. You can pick up that book on Amazon.

23. Allow for Being

I speak a lot in this book about changing, striving and doing. I give you ideas and action steps to help you move forward. However, one very important principle I have to relay to you is this idea of being.

You might find me moving away from topics you're more familiar with to something that's a bit out there. When we start talking about energy and inner work, people tend to tune out unless they're already familiar with these concepts. I'm going to try to explain them in as practical a way as possible, as if I'm talking to someone who is not wearing orange robes and doing meditation retreats in the Himalayas.

An energetic currency rules the universe. Stay with me here. We can work with it or work against it. It's much easier if you tap into the underlying universal currency of the world. It's like if you are a surfer and are surfing with the tide instead of surfing against it. If you are surfing with the tide, the ocean waves will support you. You will ride a pleasurable wave with ease and grace. However, if you're going against the tide, you will experience resistance and feel like you're going to fall off your board.

You know how much easier it is when you do things that support you and when it feels like momentum is on your side. You have tools that will help you tap into that feeling and go along with the universe. There are tools that will simply help you be who you are, without trying to do a whole lot.

For doers and achievers, doing less and "being work" is hard. If you find this chapter to be harder than the others because it requires you to do less and be more, then challenge yourself to focus more on being than on doing.

As I dealt with my own struggles and experienced resistance in doing the things I was supposed to be doing, I noticed how I was pushing against the tide. It felt like I was climbing uphill. It seemed like I had been trying to do creative work for a long time but I was tired. I was pushing things uphill and facing a lot of resistance with minimal success. I was tired of forcing things and tired of going against the resistance.

In working through my own issues with resistance, I realized that what I wasn't doing was nothing. Yes, I actually wasn't spending time not doing anything. Also, I was using primarily my brain and my mind to do all the heavy lifting. This isn't a problem unless your mind sabotages you in all the ways I have talked about in this book.

Action and effort alone may not be enough to fight the internal resistance that comes up. You need more tools. One of those tools is doing less, as I talked about in previous chapters. You need rest and downtime so you can replenish your energy, go within and come out with a bigger gust of energy. When you don't do things for some time, you can recuperate, relax and rebuild the energy you require for your next project. If you haven't taken a break in a while, or haven't taken consistent breaks, take them. Take some days off. Take some downtime and schedule weekly time to reflect and re-gather.

You don't have to put as much stress on your mind as you are. You are constantly asking your mind questions and giving it problems to solve. Give your mind time to relax and process. Give your mind time to find peace. Your mind is on a treadmill at all times. To slow down your mind and become the watcher of it, try a journaling or meditation practice. Both allow you to watch the thoughts that are going through your mind. When you watch your thoughts instead of being your thoughts, your life becomes less heavy. You don't have to carry around all the processing and calculation that your mind is doing. Even if you do, you can see that your mind is doing it. You have a little breathing room when you see that you and your mind are not one and the same.

To get out of your head, try physical activity. It doesn't matter what kind of exercise you do or what sport you play. The best part about athletics is that when your heart rate increases, you tend to focus entirely on your body and the exercise at hand. You're not thinking about all the problems, obstacles or issues in your life. When you're trying to catch your breath, you have no choice but to be present. No one ever feels like getting exercise in the beginning. If you think of exercise as another tool to help you break through the lethargy and resistance, you'll start appreciating your workouts and even get healthier in the process.

I don't know how to describe harnessing your energy and harmonizing your spirit but I'm going to try. Within you is energy that can help you move forward and get things done. There's a deep vibration of energy that you can feel or maybe see as a color. Close your eyes and try to feel the energy within you. It could be your heartbeat. It could be a strong feeling or a sense of energetic presence. I want you to notice this energy space, feel the vibrating energy and harness it. Store up this energy and keep it readily available for doing tasks.

If it's not coming through as energy, it could be coming through as spirit. You are touching the spiritual world when you walk in nature, see something beautiful, are mesmerized by a baby or feel the presence of the divine. Do you check in with your inner spiritual nature? If not, are there things that help you feel more spiritual? Does yoga or meditation help you tap into your spiritual side? Does nature or hiking help? Does going to a temple or church help? Listening to music or to a sermon? There are so many ways to tap into your spirituality. I'm encouraging you to find the thing that evokes your spirituality and to do it on a regular basis.

I grew up going to bhajan classes. This is essentially a type of Indian group choir singing practice. We sang songs to worship the divine. When I hear these songs, an inner spirit awakens. During the early part of the day, I try to listen to these songs on YouTube to put myself in a more spiritual place. When I'm listening to this music, I am not listening from my mind but, rather, from my heart and soul-center.

If you are familiar with your spirit practice, it's time for you to schedule it into your life. Our spiritual lives are just as important as all the other parts of our lives but the spiritual life is the one that we give the least attention to each day. Spend 5 to 10 minutes a day cultivating any kind of spiritual practice. Don't put this off until the end of the day (as I have done on occasion) because it's the easiest thing to avoid or forget.

Being in a spiritual place helps give you the energy you might be missing. It might awaken powers to help you pursue your goals and objectives with your project. Your spiritual nature enlivens and awakens but only if you give yourself space and time to evoke it in your life.

24. Use "No" as Your Superpower

Since I left law practice and started working with this NGO, I've had many opportunities to switch jobs. I've seen jobs that I've been qualified for, I've seen jobs that have had more responsibility and that have paid more. I've received job offers and invitations to apply for jobs, and I would have gotten certain jobs if I had applied for them. Yet, I stayed away from them because of all the things I have talked about in this book.

I've asked you to look at your principles, your purpose, your meaning, your reasons for doing what you do, your why and so on. Now, the way to stay in alignment with that is to say "no." Over and over, you have to say "no" to the life you don't want so that you can create the life you do want. I talked about this previously a bit in the chapter about going small in life. Saying "no" really shouldn't be about living a small life. You say "no" to avoid the life you don't want and to start living a more intentional life.

If you don't say "no" regularly, you allow other people to run your life. You allow yourself to fall into the trap of what everyone else is doing. You allow yourself to face distractions. You allow others to pull you in many directions. To say "no" more easily, over the last number of years, I've had to go somewhat into a "monk" mode and stay more to myself. I've stayed farther away from family and friends so I could work on my writing and my dreams. I've been very intentional about what I've said "yes" to and I have used "no" as my superpower to continue doing the work I want to do.

I can't go out on weekday evenings because that's when I do my work. I can't go out every Friday and Saturday evening because I'm pursuing my dreams. It's a sacrifice I make to create the life I want. You create the life you want by saying "no" to all the things you don't want. Go out of your way and disengage from people, activities, television shows and things you do on a regular basis that take away a chunk of your time. If you go out every Friday and Saturday night because that's what you've always done, put a stop to that. Don't let your time run away from you by default because you're spending it unconsciously.

Get more conscious about your time, your company and your energy. The world is trying to draw you away from your dreams. Other people are not sure what they are doing with their lives and they are going along with whatever is happening that weekend. Don't look for things that are happening. Look at what is happening with what you're working on and put all your focus and attention on that. Prioritize your time, your projects and your efforts. If others want your time or presence, make an exception for them. Don't spend all your time on what others want, unconsciously socializing and ending up having to make exceptions for yourself.

If you keep your life principles, your life purpose and your "why" front and center, it becomes easier to say "no." It's not that you're saying no for the sake of being difficult or a malcontent. You're simply living in alignment with the life you want. If you believe certain things and want certain things, would you spend your money on other things? If you wanted to go on a vacation, would you spend your money on upgrading your car and kitchen? Let's say you had limited funds. If you did, you would put all your money into that vacation you wanted. Why is it different with time? Put your time and energy into what you desire, not into obligations and distractions.

Check in with your purpose and your "why" every time you have to make a decision about doing something new or going to a social event. I'm not saying to give up everything and become a monk. Just be more intentional and conscious of what you're saying "yes" to. Of course you're going to attend Thanksgiving and your nephew's birthday party but maybe you're not going to attend the Super Bowl party or do the Friday night bar hopping. Or maybe you're going out to the bars with your friends but just not every weekend. Maybe you're picking and choosing.

When you receive an invitation to something, check in with your schedule. See if you have time to schedule other people in. Will doing this activity distract you or take you hours away from what you need to accomplish for the week? Finally, check in with your intuition. Does this feel right to do? Ask yourself if you actually want to do this. Would it feel good if you did this? Your gut or instincts should help you evaluate your decision pretty quickly. Give yourself a minute or two to check in with yourself before you offer an immediate or obligatory yes.

Two tendencies to keep in mind are people-pleasing and community obligations. Notice whether you're practicing any of these habits; if you are, become more mindful of them. You may say "yes" more than you want because you don't want to disappoint other people. You want to make them happy. Yet you do this at the cost of your own sanity, boundaries and limits. If you don't want to do something, be truthful to yourself. Please yourself first instead of making others happy. Don't show up to events and be part of activities where others are happy and you're resentful. Notice that your desire to make others happy is coming at the expense of your own happiness.

Also, notice community obligations whose premise is reciprocity. As a society, we tend to find ourselves obligated quite a bit under the premise of "I'll do for you what you do for me." This is good in some respects, in terms of keeping friendships and family connections strong, but be more intentional about it. Don't do everything other people want you to do just because they'll show up for your own dinner party or event. Be more mindful when you're doing things out of obligation. Tell yourself or acknowledge when you're doing something out of obligation or to return a favor. Be more aware that when you're inviting people to do things, you may feel obligated to attend their event in the future.

I'm stressing the importance of saying "no" because it really is the superpower that activates many of the other ideas I talk about in this book. To stay focused, efficient and moving towards what you want, you need a tool to help you stay far away from those things that are sucking up your energy and time. That tool is "no." You must be mindful of the default and convenient life so that you can choose the life of your own creation. You must be careful about distracting yourself and letting others pull you away from what it is you want to be doing. Your job is to keep your eyes on the prize, focus on your desires and stay in alignment with your dreams.

Get Off the Floor and Get Going

We are almost at the end here. I hope you're not exhausted by this quick ride we've taken together.

I've been just as stuck as you are, just as procrastinating as you are and just as inefficient as you have been at times.

For some of us, the feelings of productivity and efficiency come and go. They're neither constant nor consistent.

Those of us who are tasked with creating, starting, building and opening have trouble doing so because of what's going on within us.

If you feel stuck, I urge you to explore what is it that's keeping you stuck.

First and foremost, is this work that you're trying to do in alignment with your skills and values? Is this the work you're supposed to be doing in the world?

If it is in alignment with who you are and what you're supposed to be doing, what's preventing you from doing it?

Getting clear on the thing that's keeping you stuck is the most important thing you can do to get unstuck. Getting to that root cause, the root fear or the deeper block between you and the goal you want to achieve will help you break free of the thing that is holding you back.

I hope you not only inquire why but also implement some of the many strategies I've talked about in this book.

Different methods of overcoming procrastination and motivation may work for different people.

One idea may work for you today while another idea may work for you tomorrow.

For years, my fears paralyzed me, as did my unfounded worries about things that didn't matter. Then I decided to get up off the floor, sit down and go to work.

The thing with motivation is that it builds on momentum.

When you are slightly motivated and start working on the thing you're supposed to be doing, small achievements and goals inspire you to do more.

Ten minutes turns into 10 hours.

You can do this. You got this.

Each time I've gone through long periods of unproductivity, I've worked with coaches who helped me break out of those places in my life.

Just identifying the block has opened the floodgate of productivity and motivation. I can be truly motivated and productive when I realize what it is that is holding me back.

About the Author

Vishnu is the author of *7 Sacred Promises: A Practical Guide for Living With Meaning and Purpose and One-Way Ticket: 11 Ways to Discover Your Highest Purpose and Transition Out of Your Profession.*

He is the blogger behind the popular relationship and personal growth blog, Vishnu's Virtues, as well as his motivational blog on Medium, where he writes about getting unstuck and motivated in life.

Vishnu also coaches people who are struggling to pursue their goals and dreams in life. He helps them get unstuck, motivated and on the path to achieving the life they want.

Before writing and coaching, Vishnu practiced criminal, family and immigration law. While he enjoyed helping people navigate the justice system, it wasn't his true life's purpose. He left the law field and pursued his calling to inspire others through his writing and coaching.

To keep up with Vishnu's weekly posts, please visit his Medium blog
https://medium.com/@VishnusVirtues

You can find his books on his Amazon page
https://www.amazon.com/Vishnus-Virtues/e/B00XH077L0

For the Vishnu's Virtues blog on relationships, visit:
www.vishnusvirtues.com

For Vishnu's book, *Is God Listening?*, visit
https://gumroad.com/l/EXBba

For Vishnu's book, *One Way Ticket*, visit
https://gumroad.com/l/UTdv

Vishnu on Instagram:
https://www.instagram.com/innermotivation_vishnu

For constructive feedback, questions or coaching, email me at
vishnusvirtues@gmail.com